SIGN POSTS

A COLLECTION OF ESSAYS

Volume I

ii

Other Books by Don Davison

An Outline of a Philosophy of the Consciousness of Truth
The Concept of Personhood in the Evolutionary Process of Being
The Game of Life: A Player's Manual for Executives and Others
Sign Posts: A Collection of Essays, Vol. II
Sign Posts: A Collection of Essays, Vol. III

Poetry

Thoughts and Feelings Book I
Thoughts and Feelings Book II
Needles from the Ponderosas at Zirahuen
Seeds from the Ponderosas at Zirahuen
Pitch from the Ponderosas at Zirahuen
Humus from the Ponderosas at Zirahuen
Sawdust from the Ponderosas at Zirahuen
Sun's rays through the Ponderosas at Zirahuen
Shadows beneath the Ponderosas at Zirahuen
Cones from the Ponderosas at Zirahuen
Pollen sifting from the Ponderosas at Zirahuen
Reflections from Lucerne
Searching Swamps
Questions
Time's Echoes
Memories

Collections

Always Extolling
Murmurings
Iris and Other Things
Pieces of the Journey
Through the Swamps of Time

SIGN POSTS

A COLLECTION OF ESSAYS

Volume I

Don Davison

Zirahuen
Phoenix, AZ
pathtotheself.com
DrDavison@pathtotheself.com

©2010 by Zirahuen
All rights reserved. Published 2010
Printed in the United States of America

ISBN 978-0-9774039-4-3

Cover photo and author photo by Patricia Davison

Special thanks to Louella Holter, formerly with the Bilby Research Center of Northern Arizona University, and to Tina Rosio, from W.

Again –
To Patricia, for everything.

All of Don Davison's books have water on their covers. Water is one of the most essential attributes of the planet Earth; without it, life as we know it would not exist. It deserves our most considered attention.

Davison's collections of poetry all end with "Finding Pieces." Many of you have asked, where did the rules for the Game of Life come from? They come from many places and different times. Good hunting!

CONTENTS OF THIS VOLUME
SIGN POSTS I

CONTENTS OF
SIGN POSTS II

CONTENTS OF
SIGN POSTS III

AUTHOR'S NOTE

I am primarily a poet; these essays are intended to help "flesh out" various themes and topics found in my poetry. Where I feel it is appropriate, I might refer you, dear reader, to a particular poem that further elucidates certain thoughts or sentiments. These and other materials are marked with an asterisk. If not otherwise noted, such inclusions are my own work.

PREFACE

Sign Posts are collections of essays written to shed some light on my personal thinking. Over the years, students and others have asked that I write some small pieces on what I felt about this or that. In the following working pieces called "postings," I will attempt to share some of the fundamental points of departure that have guided my thinking and stimulated my searching in my various fields of interest. These pieces will be augmented with the new and intriguing that I find as I continue to discover the richness of the human garden and the unfathomable depths of the human experience.

I believe that "as a species, we must act in love (in that Frommian manner: with an active concern for all life and growth) by operating and proceeding with knowledge, care, responsibility, and respect while we dedicate ourselves to growth as self and circumstances change. We must live with the awareness that a sanctifying process is always underway" (from *A Word About Politics*, in this current edition).

A HUMAN FACE – A HUMAN TOUCH

As we step into the next millennium,
awash in the wake of the post industrial,
postmodern,
electronic media-saturated environment,
we must be ever vigilant.
Evolution has taken such a wonderfully
long time to get us here –
through interstellar trails
of primeval dust and muck.
Now,
thresholding into the future
as co-participants in the creative process,
we are faced, as always,
with the opportunity to maintain an
ever-present commitment
to what personhood is all about.
A fleeting incessant blip
on our intellectual, emotional, physical,
and spiritual horizons
hints of an unknown presence shadowing us.
Something always has –
perhaps the gods,
or evil spirits?
Now that "God is Dead"[*] and evil spirits are
the entertainment of children and teenagers,
what is it that blows the winds of turbulence,
shakes our tree,
shadows our sunny days?
What eclectic movements do we fear?
What dissonance absorbs our senses?

---

[*] As headlined by *Time Magazine* and others.

The venues of the day's exposure
come from an implosion of people
(other beings present in our known space)
and data coming from everywhere,
overloading all of our senses.
Numbers,
beyond the simple,
are incomprehensible
(except to a few)
and therefore without our comprehension, meaningless.
Yet ...
the presence of others,
different others,
(only in that naive historical sense)
is disconcerting.
We don't feel connected.
Something tells us we should,
we are all brothers and sisters,
and yet ...
we really aren't quite sure
how we go about that magnanimous interface.
In any case,
we have too much on our plates.
And the banter,
informative and noxious of all kinds,
soothes, assaults,
and otherwise floods our commuting time
while punctuations of music/noise
occupies our ears and boom-boxes
carried on four wheels
invade personal space, causing disturbing sensations.

Is any of this understandable,
or are we all by default
"buying"
the postmodern dissonance as the only truth?
If it sells, it must be good.
The truth has become a market-driven commodity,
hasn't it?
Projectiles of jacketed lead death abound,
methods of delivery are available through mail order
to almost everyone.
Tons of ordnance
(the equivalent of so much TNT)
including those insidious antipersonnel land mines
still lie scattered about
as we wander aimlessly into tomorrow
surrounded by the omnipresent
Data Smog[*] of the day.
To whom can we turn for answers?
Where can we look for that special interface,
that process called higher formal
(does formal have meaning any more?)
education
and see a human face and feel a human touch?
It must be more or less than virtual reality
(now that's an oxymoron).
Something is either real as a creation, or invention,
that although "real"
isn't "really real."
Ah, but who can tell?
Some say it is and maybe they are right.
And I don't want to be embarrassed with my ignorance.

---

[*] *Data Smog,* by David Shenk.

God knows
(That's only a figure of speech, now, of course)
I don't know everything.
But I do, at some level, know what I think I like.
So ...
when I think about it
(that pastime of reflecting with an honest wonder)
"It,"
sharing being in time
(real now-time for most of us)
must,
if we reflect long enough about
our *real* comfort zone
(with self and others),
be doable, rewarding, and regenerating.
It all must be more than media
transformed into a medium
becoming a message.
It must be a transubstantial exercise
of shared being
melting into one
and that one,
for most of us,
must have predominantly real time,
real life attributes.
Our universities for the next millennium must be personal.
They cannot be too cold,
they must be warm enough.
They cannot be too hard,
they must be soft enough.

4

We are that rational social animal,
the homofaber, the destroyer,
the freedom seeker,
a symbolizing,
soul-seeking sentient being
who in the courses of our species' journey
must forever size personhood to itself.
We must be very close
(close enough)
to who we *really* are,
not simulacra ad nauseam.
After all,
how many of me can there *really* be?
Just one!
We know the "times they are a'changin."
So they have been saying and so they are,
and yet
as each ripple on the pond
disturbs the serenity of our aspirations,
we feel more than a little anxious.
Echoes in the winds of time
repeat the age-old rational/social dictum:
How much is too much and how much is too little?
To this, we must pay attention.
We (some of us) have bought
at the physical level
the "use it or lose it" mandate.
Now we *MUST* extend this commitment to the other three
theaters
of our personhoods:
the intellectual, emotional and spiritual.
So we may ask …
How many tools do we need and of what kind?
At what pace must we labor and for what purpose?

To whom and to what do we dedicate our very best
as we attempt to share the knowledge of the ages
so that we may enhance our Now?
Are we able to protect ourselves and our children
from donning victimhoods of our blind machinations,
as the Internet's tentacles gather in force and kind?
The answer *MUST* be a forever yes!
Yes! And yes again!
To ignore the hard-won wisdom of history is more than foolish,
it is life threatening and not just to us here now,
but to all those children here now,
"the forever young that come and come and come,"[*]
wide eyed and innocent,
truly victims.
We *MUST* choose not to sacrifice them on some altar
of the marketplace.
We must touch them and look into their faces and say,
"Yes! Yes! And yes again!"
Yes! To the beauty of each one!
Yes! To the doability of our *real selves*!
Yes! To the current crown of humanity
with its multicolored, multilingual, multicultural,
multifaceted personhood!

---

[*] "Reap the Wind," from *Always Extolling*.

A NEW POINT OF DEPARTURE

As a social species, we have always had to live *as if* new truths were to become an essential part of our survival. Now, even though we know there will be inconsistencies, some dramatic and astonishing, others shameful, in our repertoire of survival skills, the worst and most recent – the ineptitude in intervening in the Balkans, Cambodia, Rwanda, and Darfur, as well as the corruptive intransigence at all levels – are obvious.

Wrapped as we have been and will forever be in the environ of the moment, we must continue to live by trusting in that organic nature of the learning process. In this vein, we need to know that there is a learning curve for creators and destroyers as well as victims and interveners. The implications of this fact carry a universal responsibility that cannot turn us from our course of commitment, and an unerring faith must guide our resolve. If we are to continue to live, we must live *as if* all life matters.

An understanding of an organic process of human growth and development must be promulgated and adhered to so that the evolution of the species continues to manifest in its self-understanding a more universal rise in consciousness.

Appropriate communication becomes the most profound attribute of being human. Purveying essential information is an absolute. The more prepared the general populace is to fathom universal truths, the shorter the time frame will be leading to a deeper understanding of the beauty as well as the danger of

those truths. Essential in the ever-increasing body of new comprehensions is the innate value of each person. This new depth
of enlightenment and commitment will produce a sharper
focus, generating the necessary momentum to not only follow a
new course, but also to choose to stay that course.

Staying the course will allow us to maintain the desired
commitment to sustain our new focus, and it will also give us
the necessary understanding that all things take some measure
of time. Farming knows sowing, and reaping manifests the
prudence of patience that understands time.* Our species'
current understanding of "the new physics" notwithstanding,
for us human beings, is being is – being human over time.

Given the significance of new truths, electorates – and this
includes all of us – must identify the cowardly who cannot
assume the responsibility of action and enlighten or eliminate
them from their positions of ignorance and obstructionism. The
obvious fact that the process of life is 24/7 now pervades the
consciousness of the vast majority of the human family and
with this new enlightenment comes a new responsibility. That
fact's existential mandate must be clear enough to demand
sufficient focus on not only the continuity of life, but also the
blossoming of the great human potential. In general, for most
members of the human family, the political consensus carries
sufficient common sense that we now recognize the need to
default to the protection of all human life, indeed all manner of
life.

In our former state of ignorance, many times we waited too
long and upon occasion have not responded at all to the cries of
agony and pain coming from all corners of the globe. With our

---

* See "A Farm," as well as "Wait!" and "Hope," in *Iris and Other Things.*

new knowledge of the integrated whole, ignorance and lack of action is no longer an option. As new life presents itself in all of its splendid glory we must open our minds, hearts, and arms to embrace a new understanding of a *presence of being* that brings with it new and profound realities. Growth is that ever-present gift of new knowledge that leads us towards a greater understanding of ourselves and the other.

A WORD ABOUT POLITICS ...

Politics is holding on to ourselves and stepping into the next moment, realizing that we are always our own responsibility. This demands reflection and self-ownership – thinking with integrity, speaking with integrity, and doing with integrity. This exemplifies truth – our truth.

Always sprinting to some finish line, rushing all over to be seen and heard by everyone, creates the impression that we are ill prepared to take care of ourselves, our families, our work, and our friends, much less a nation.

Owning one's self in real time for our sake and the sake of everyone else is a measured and considered endeavor. In the Polis, one must live with the integrity of self and this can only be done in that self-reflection of self-ownership. One must always be parsing the truth of all that one knows by owning it and knowing that "it and I are one." A good way to do this is to repeat *true/not true – mine/not mine*[*] as a prayerful mantra.

We must act in love by operating and proceeding with *knowledge, care, responsibility, and respect* while dedicating ourselves to growth as selves and circumstances change. We must live with the awareness that a sanctifying process is always underway.

We must not scurry about slipping and falling – bumping into self and others (especially the children), while creating and

---

[*] See "The Rules" in *The Game of Life: A Player's Manual for Executives and Others.*

11

babbling nonsense. We must live in this sacred crucible of life by always stepping into each new day with the integrity of a conscious, growing self-knowledge and understanding that must be shared with all others of the human family. This sharing must always be done with the integrity inherent in the process of an unfolding creation. We must own what we know by doing all that we are.

GROW UP, AMERICA!

The current state of muddled thinking that abounds in the minds of some, and I think this could safely be said of many U.S. citizens, has become manifest in much of the so-called "leadership" and the media of the day. The conversations of many of its citizens (used advisedly), as well as many of their actions, or lack thereof as individuals and as a nation, have demonstrated an immaturity that at times has made it the laughingstock of the enlightened members of the human family, or as well, a target for those so inclined.

The thinness of our current national dialog has been adolescent and borders on the childish. This must be seen as an advisedly problematic circumstance, given the lack of a depth of understanding of many of our citizens about current and historical national affairs. A decidedly shallow commitment to an active participation in the governing of the Republic and that Republic's participation in global affairs, is also manifest. The United States has a poor record of actively seeking sufficient participation in and understanding of current national and international affairs. Voicing informed opinions that are shared via participation in a rational national dialog is an essential attribute of a healthy nation. The current lack of participation in local, state, and federal elections does not bode well for the life of the nation.

A Brief Historical Perspective

Yes, there was a "birth" of a nation. Yes, that nation spent time, and still does, manifesting its destiny. And yes, it wanted, and to some degree still does, to be left alone to "do its own thing." All of these are historically understandable attributes of a nation in its childhood. This nation, although birthed by enlightened forefathers and foremothers, did not then have the current global circumstance (exploding numbers of individuals and rampant applications of technology) on its plate. Now it must live in the current moment. Our history, as well as the history of all others, abounds in facts. These facts must be understood in context and they cannot be used as excuses.

The United States has an excellent opportunity, along with the responsibility to pass along the same sound values that were espoused by its dedicated nation creators, to its future generations. It is only with well-informed participating citizens that a nation can hope to survive. How are we doing? One side of the coin of liberty is an informed electorate consenting to act responsibly. This is the opportunity side of that coin and it is still shining in its beauty and plenitude. The other side, that more mature side, the one that bespeaks a reciprocal responsibility as concomitant to opportunity, is not so bright. Responsibility is always first to self and then to others. As children of the enlightenment, it took the United States a civil war, many clashes of cultures (indigenous and imported), along with slave labor and an industrial revolution to fathom some of the depths of the earth-shaking humanitarian implications of its founding ideals. It was not a journey of a few years (think Afghanistan, Iraq, parts of Asia, as well as parts of Africa, Russia, Venezuela, and elsewhere). Indeed, we and the rest of the global family still labor at the humanitarian task.

Whatever excuses the citizenry may wish to employ in apologetics for the worst of our behaviors or our lack of understanding of the current state of affairs, none of them serve the country in good stead in honestly understanding either some of its early history, or some of its participation in the 19th, 20th, and 21st centuries. That the nation needed to move from a childhood nation to an adolescent nation, and then to embark on becoming a maturing young nation, is understood. It has had a childhood and an adolescence of sufficient lengths. They have been filled with robust accomplishments, and with the pitfalls of ignorance and rampant energy unbridled by seasoned experience. This circumstance must eventually give way to some reflective repose that in its mulling makes for a deeper understanding, leading to a greater depth and breadth of responsibility that must manifest itself first to self and then to others.

Yes, we know there have been world wars and grand ideologies. Yes, there have been the tribal and religious cloaks that, while protecting harbored inhibitions, were in many cases less than helpful. There has always been the friction of interface between cultures with different languages, customs, religions, and a sense of space. We are now beset with a different level of awareness – of a global oneness that challenges us to new understandings of the flow of history – all history. Intelligence is where you find it, and as such is a resource for itself and the world (think especially of women). To foster and protect it is a global privilege and sacred responsibility.

The developmental profile of the United States has always carried with it a certain reticence when it comes to regional relations and the affairs of other nations, that is, unless there was some advantage to be had, an advantage that bespoke at times a certain lack of magnanimity towards others of different stock. Now, while prudence is a virtue, pontificating values that one is not willing, ready, and able to espouse bespeaks a lack of maturity and commitment. Grand eloquence also gives a measure of the person. The bravado of adolescent ignorance becomes intolerable as mature behavior is expected and not forthcoming.

Our Current Circumstance

Insights about processing information or the lack thereof are given by our own Samantha Power in her telling book *A Problem from Hell*. On page 89, quoting Prince Sirik Matak, she writes, "As for you and in particular for your great country, I never believed for a moment that you would [abandon] a people which has chosen liberty. You have refused us your protection and we can do nothing about it … If I shall die here on this spot in my country that I love … I have only committed this mistake of believing in you, the Americans." Again, on page 121 she describes a lack of willingness to know and to commit to established tenets, which leads to a failure to act accordingly. In speaking of Cambodia, she says, "With the country sealed tight, statesmen and citizens [hardly many] could take shelter in the fog of plausible deniability. However, even once they accepted the information, the moral implications of that information did not really sink in. For those back in Washington, 10,000 miles from the refugee camps at the Thai border, it would take years to promote the raw, unconfirmed data to the status of knowledge."

One can now think "and Darfur, all of Sudan, etc." … the list is long. It would be extremely hard to make a case that at some of these recent junctures in human history, there was insufficient information present to understand the kinds of atrocities that can be, are being, and will be perpetrated by members of our species. Nor would it be easy to make a case that we shoulder no responsibility for those victims of madness.

We now know the only mature response is to own what we know. If we were, as a nation, to take responsibility for what we know, when we know it, we would be exuding a measure of that reflective repose so necessary to a maturing mantle that must be worn with a forthright commitment to espoused beliefs. Our national record to date is less than acceptable. It is not difficult to say that in many ways it is deplorable. From our naïve and unacceptable position, many times we have failed to seek sufficient information to understand the global whole, as well as many of its parts.

While we cannot rewrite history, certainly we can be aware of writing current history with our own actions. The fundamentals of our constitutional mindset must be embraced with a willingness to share every opportunity for freedom in all endeavors with our many neighbors of the world. (China, Russia, Iran, North Korea, Venezuela, and others, please pay attention!) At this time, we must know that a continuing litany of quotes from a Bill of Rights, or a Constitution, although meaningful, is less than sufficient. The historical unwillingness to commit, the shallowness of understanding, the general lack of interest in "others," and a naïve point of departure for involvement (intended and unintended) in the affairs of other states, along with an unacceptable sustained ignorance toward the effects of that involvement, are all telltale signs of an adolescent mindset. This adolescent mindset has lasted sufficiently long to get the citizenry and the nation into serious trouble. An adolescent encumbered with ignorance, avarice, and pride, as all adolescence is, cannot serve itself well, much less a nation. The United States is playing a part on a global stage that requires a greater depth of enlightened participation.

The time has come for the citizens to choose to emancipate themselves from a prolonged adolescence. As with all life, we must choose responsible maturation or die. The United States has reveled far too long in an adolescence that was grand, but now finally must end. It is time for the citizens of the United States to look around and to appreciate the depth and magnitude of the great human undertaking. If this means that we must go abroad, then we must. This nation was not founded on an aggressive policy of ideological imperialism. It was, however, notably committed to espousing the freedoms of freedom. To do this we must be prepared to offer a hand to those who are oppressed and downtrodden. Being a neighbor to one's own is always a current challenge. Every United States hamlet and megapolis, as well as many other parts of the world, is bursting with opportunities to be a neighbor to one's own as well as to the world at large. Although the saying "Love begins at home" is still true, it has always also been true that "if true – then true, if love at all – then love of all."

That there are many different people in the world is more than self-evident. Some have basic survival needs that they are unable to meet. Some are held captive by tribal infrastructures that are ill equipped to deal with vast geographies and millions of people. Some live in places that are not blessed with an abundance of natural resources that could enable their culture to have the surplus necessary for a greater level of freedom, reflection, and creativity. "From those who are blessed, much is asked." This obvious truism must be understood and owned.

The people of the United States, along with many other nations, have been undeniably blessed. The United States, along with those other nations, consumes a greater proportionate share of global abundance. That this circumstance continues, one could argue, is merely an adherence to the laws of physics:

Bodies in motion stay in motion. Yet, to be callous to those with legitimate needs speaks with less than a mature heart. It manifests the ignorance of an adolescent who has not had sufficient time to become informed and to own a new knowledge, based upon an increase in information and the integration of that information in an expanding worldview.

It must also be said: The United States' generosity is legendary and along with other nations so inclined has done heroic things. What is being said here is that there have always been those difficulties that simmer beneath the surface; it is to a greater world-view that we must all aspire. We cannot rest on laurels already won.

Historically there have always been those lone voices. Kipling spoke of obligations: "Of the white man's burden." This has now become the burden of any nation of means. At this juncture in the human epic it must be eminently clear that unnecessary suffering does not have to be a given. Again, this is not to say that the United States and many other nations have done nothing. It is precisely because so many have done so much that we must honestly press on with a commitment that espouses every measure of husbanding resources well, by making those necessary sacrifices of personnel and material in times of need.

Freedom is not free. It must be maintained with blood, sweat, and tears. We must now maintain a new level of awareness and we must remember that new opportunities abound for an enlightened participation in a shared global presence. That this sharing presence will cause the deaths of some is a given. That that number should be understood to be a diminishing necessity must also be understood. Life and growth is about birth and death. As a greater abundance of knowledge is shared and understood, fewer people will be needlessly sacrificed on the altar of ignorance. No nation has the right to be a bystander in the process of life – any life. We are "the conscious species" and as such, must bear that burden, a burden that when borne well leads to countless gifts of life to life.

The United States is a young Republic, as the world goes, and must own its own history, its place in world history, and its commitments to the ideals that gave birth to the nation. The understanding of that history, of the consequences of our heroic acts – as well as of intended and unintended errors of judgment – must be part of any current national as well as international perspective of integrated growth and development.

As a nation, "we the people" of the United States do not have all the answers. Consider a recent survey of UNICEF entitled *A comprehensive assessment of the lives and well-being of children and adolescents in the economically advanced nations. UNICEF Innocenti Research Centre Report Card 7.* The United States ranks very close to the bottom. This should come as an indictment to those who know and do not do. It should also shame us and serve as a national rallying cry for a young, maturing nation, knowing that its future lies always with the young.

All growth is a leading out, *educere*, education. How are we doing? At the level of rhetoric, "no child left behind," we have the message and yet the essential commitment to follow through is still lagging. As looked at by many measures we could do much better. Accomplishments do not need to be set in some naïve utopia where zero tolerance is the only acceptable goal. We must accept an organic model where close enough is always close enough only when we do our very best, and that of necessity we must always press on. We must continue to commit to an ever-diminishing number of neglected and forgotten children. Sure, the United States is a large nation. Yes, there are large numbers of children in and out of schools and yes, we do have an immigration problem. None of these can be seen or used as excuses. We have sufficient resources, in both personnel and dollars, to address all of these issues.

What keeps the United States from making a national commitment through local commitments to do the very best for all of its citizens as well as for others? This topic has been a perennial issue since the times of our founders when they recognized that any commitment must be first to self and then to others. They foresaw a time when no segment of the population would be deprived of essential freedoms. To them it was obvious that only through education could a nation be sound and prosper. We have prospered almost beyond belief and have pursued our given goals. We have not, as of yet, set the nation's priorities in order. That we have progressed is certainly beyond any doubt; where we lack in our accomplishment is in maintaining a sufficient focus on the responsibility for the essentials.

This being the case, education at all levels and on every subject must receive a greater degree of attention from every quarter. Education cannot be a thin slice of an ever-thinner slice of the past. An honest appraisal of where we have been, what we did and did not do, what we are doing, or are not, and what we should and should not be doing must form the template for an honest expression of personhood and nationhood.

As a percent of GDP, relative to military expenditures, the United States is not allocating sufficient resources to enable the nation as a whole to participate responsibly in its growth and development. This does not mean we should spend less on the development of appropriate military personnel and resources.

That the world can be a most unfriendly place is a fact. Nor does this mean that throwing money at problems solves them. What must occur here is that we hear that tried and true mandate: "It must be done with heart and soul." The entire citizenry must be galvanized to an acceptance of a communal responsibility. This requires a paradigm shift towards what we must now acknowledge is true: We have not allocated sufficient resources or time and that all-important commitment of "heart and soul" to the oversight necessary to monitor governmental expenditures in every endeavor. The United States has historically had more to allocate and consequently must monitor more actively an honest use of those resources. Waste is never something to be proud of, or something we can ignore.

All social infrastructures must be maintained regularly and must be improved upon to become more efficient, or eliminated where they are no longer needed. We now know that we are a part of the organic whole and must take our cues from the process itself. As Nature moves, we must pay attention to our participation in the process. This demands an ever-vigilant posture and wisdom commensurate with our experience.

In the "think," "say," "do," of our conscious presence it's those choices that coincide with free and open purpose that build the character of individuals and of nations. It is in etiquette, those manners, the ones we call "right stuff," that we are guided to restful graves, where whispers of "well done" slip silently into time.

IMMIGRATION – A BRIEF HISTORY

Immigration is the story of human life. Our habits of roaming and settling have led us from being tribal and regional to members of states, and finally to some sense of national and global cohesion. This wanderlust coincided with a felt need, a fundamental aspect of our behavior, a natural right.

Now, in our species' history, we know that there is no space left on earth that is not occupied by some national or international jurisdiction. Where does this place us as individuals? Our past and present wanderings have taught us much about the world, others, and ourselves. In the beginning we espoused values that we came to believe worked for us, whether they were values of myth, religion, or custom. We took these values with us wherever we went.

Time and our own development have taught us that some of what we believed was not true. The accumulation of information from all corners of the globe and from all the peoples of the world came to present itself as a new science. This science of nature and our place in it emerged, enlarged, and integrated a much more thorough view of the world and of humankind. Eventually most of us became aware of the fact that whether we spoke a particular language or believed in a particular religion or custom, this growing awareness was not without its faults. Our continued presence on the planet was determined by circumstances that dictated the potential for survival.

In the course of events, we created governments to protect us from ourselves and from others of our own kind. We must now learn to apply governmental circumstances that have the potential to maintain safe, productive living opportunities for us all. Finally, we have come to know that which is lethal for one of us can be lethal for all of us. Fangs and poisons of the flora and fauna as well as disease and weaponry of every ilk know no boundary. Most of us have also come to know that to be nations of equanimity birthing magnanimity we must be nations of laws and we must aggressively enforce those laws.

There are similarities in our social conventions and natural law. We have also learned that there is a need to model our laws after the consequences of our human interests and behaviors. I want to address the current state of immigration based upon this natural propensity of the species to be wanderers. Indeed, wandering has proven to be efficacious for us all. In light of the success of our natural history, I also would like to offer an organic model of governance.

From this frame of reference, we must understand that Nature's model for governing all circumstances, including social circumstances, demands an omnipresent maintenance of the certain beneficial behaviors that have resulted in our survival. Laws of survival became the ideals and guiding principles of all given populations. The conscious obedience of these ideals and laws became what we call personhood. By this, I mean personhood is the culmination of behavioral patterns that formed what may be viewed as an organic model for the success of human behavior – knowing and acting upon what is in our best interests.

When a critical mass (something around 80%; see note on page 36) of a population operates in the best interests of enough of the whole, there is sufficient opportunity for growth and development to sustain itself and influence others to do the same.

Personhoods of the current century have been worn for some time under slightly different circumstances, and so it is that in the current implosion of people, with or without permission, we have come to recognize the benefits of knowing who is moving about and for what purpose. Currently, this culmination of behavioral patterns forms what may be viewed as an organic model of personhood. This has served to protect the ideals and laws of people so that a shared humanitarian presence has the potential to serve most of the people. That there is a negative to this scenario is understood. Warring disagreements, a part of the global psyche, have been with us for some time. It must also be said that war in and of itself has not deterred the movement or the development of the species.

It is poetic that in the course of events, as different nations developed their own flavors of ideals and laws, an international body would attempt to capture some amalgam of multiethnic, multiracial, multireligious views and put forward a universal document. That document is the Universal Declaration of Human Rights. That there is broad appeal to this document is obvious in that the number of signatories to the international convention is 192 nations. It must also be said that, while national governments have become signatories, this does not mean that all individuals of those nations have the same sentiments.

We are still in a very dynamic, natural and developmental stage of social and ecological evolution. Meanwhile, the fact remains that we are some six billion strong. We now have more people sharing more of what we individually and corporately do than ever before in the history of the species.

Today there are covenants and constitutional writs that expound rights and obligations under penalties of law or custom. There also are some communal groups, or powerful smaller groups, who are empowered by their various constituencies to enforce laws for the ostensible good of the people. Our ongoing challenge is to further understand those rights and obligations so that a responsibility to enhance and protect them becomes a reality.

U.S. Immigration Policy

The U.S. immigration policy has much to be proud of, as well as some things that cause great concern. As a nation of immigrants, we have a past that is glorious, abhorrent, and ridiculous. While we invited those so inclined to immigrate and become a part of this great experiment in democracy, we also supported the practice of slavery and some of us, upon occasion, genocide. Overall, however, we have been extremely successful in creating a dynamic amalgam of cultures that has produced some of the best accomplishments of the species.

At this point in the history of the United States, we are being challenged with another set of circumstances that will require a consensus of the common will. In arriving at that consensus, it will be necessary to have a measure of understanding of this country's history as well as an understanding of the current social and economic fabric of other nations.

A Brief Comment

Again, it goes without saying that all human activities have always been in the "on" position. People are exercising their freedoms, governments are operating, and economies are providing goods and services. Life is ongoing. We are moving about the planet in ever-increasing numbers, depending upon what we consider to be in our best interests. This fact of human mobility, governed by some rules and regulations in the various parts of the world, has changed little over the course of human events.

The recent discussion that is taking place in the United States, in other nations, and among the international community about immigration is not about just targeting a specific group of people, but identifying some very undesirable individuals or groups. This comes to the forefront now because of a dramatic increase in numbers as well as a set of specific prevailing circumstances that threaten the lives of individuals and the workings of nations.

That there have always been "rotten apples" in every barrel is a truism. That all groups of people have attempted to organize (deal with those rotten apples) is a fact, and that people can be successful in dealing with them is also true. There are those examples in history when, for a brief period, a given group with a maligned intent has gained the upper hand. Those moments tended to be bloody and oppressive. None of them has survived any great measure of time, which bespeaks a new level of wisdom for the species. The gaining of more wisdom and its further application is ongoing. This necessitates a comment for further discussion: Technology has always provided illicit opportunities for some malignant individuals. It is obvious that with the increase in numbers and technology, they are becoming problems with serious consequences. In addition, although sometimes technology is used to monitor people and technology itself, it must be remembered that "we" are responsible for ourselves. Insufficient commitment is being made in this arena.

The Current Moment

The United States is now faced with an immigration problem that has a growing number of individuals, many of whom are currently involved in a personal and familial history that will be difficult to resolve. At what point in time did we become aware that there was a growing problem? How did we perceive the problem? What do we intend to do about it? These are all reasonable and belated questions.

To begin to attempt some meaningful answers we need to have an honest appraisal of some historical facts. Every group of immigrants has brought some new ingredients to the melting pot of our culture. This has resulted in a stew that has become ever more delicious and more substantial.

One of these groups, "the Mexicans," must be of special interest. In this case, a lengthy history spans the entire life of the United States. We are a nation that is wrapped into the history of another nation and its people. Even though the birth of the United States predates the birth of modern Mexico, there has been an intimate sharing of presences for some four hundred years. As one would assume with the natural course of events, there have been the normal sets of circumstances: Who was here first? Does it really matter? What has been the "working" history of this relationship, and not just with people but also with governmental entities?

A meaningful beginning in any attempt to understand the current circumstance must be this fact: There have been "Mexicans" here from the very beginning; most of those who were here when the transfer of sovereignty took place were excited about becoming part of a new young and growing nation. They stayed and became part of the great amalgam. However, by becoming part of a new whole, they did not abandon entirely their customs, language, or ties to their mother country. In reality, it was right under foot and right next door. This, as a mitigating factor, must be understood in order to understand the history of the "Mexican presence."

Other groups of nationalities did not have an immediate contact with their mother countries. Closeness matters. Cores of Spanish-speaking enclaves provided seedbeds for others who would later see the benefits of coming to this great nation, and they came.

The numbers were small in the beginning but they have remained steady, and over the course of time the numbers have escalated through family ties and governmental programs, such as the guest worker program, as well as nationality by birth or by relationship. This has occurred to such an extent that Mexican Americans have now become the largest minority group in the nation. In and of itself that would not matter – except that for the fact that many broke laws to get here and to stay here.

Due to a lack of oversight by state and federal authorities, or even citizen watch groups, many Mexicans who came to work on federal programs have chosen to stay in the United States illegally. Historically, many others have also chosen to come uninvited by traversing the U.S.–Mexico border. Over time, the Mexican border became a porous avenue for people from all over the world to come to the United States illegally. Does it surprise anyone that people follow others? They merely choose to take the path of historical opportunity and least resistance. During that same time, the nation was too preoccupied with other matters to deal effectively with growing numbers of illegal immigrants. Occasionally an insightful individual would broach the topic of illegal aliens but would be either put down or ignored. However, nothing in the organic disappears – it merely evolves.

Now, with substantial numbers affecting local, state, and federal resources, as well as being dangerous, people are beginning to look more closely at the issue. It has finally been perceived to be what it has been for some time, a very serious problem.

In the realm of the organic, molecules have protective membranes to screen out foreign bodies, entities that may not have the integrity of the whole in mind. No nation can survive without some measure of control over its borders. This fact is now complicated by another disturbing fact: there are individuals who, by taking advantage of the lack of sufficient controls at the borders, can easily enter this country with catastrophic purpose and intent. They and maligned applications of technology can have very serious consequences.

Given historical and actual circumstances, we immediately need to begin to undertake measures to ensure that the immigration problem is resolved. Along with this dawning of awareness comes the subsequent responsibility to resolve any connecting problems without creating problems that are more serious.

Borders and Immigration

Numbers matter. History is real. In addition, the human family has some members that do not have the well-being of some parts or of the whole in mind. Indeed, numbers are becoming more and more important. For example, the number of polluting processes in the present as well as the supportive social infrastructures bespeak a lack of understanding that portends potential problems of great magnitude for the individual as well as the whole. That history is connected to the present is obvious.

Our Spanish-speaking relatives are just that – relatives. We must be more than a little understanding of their circumstance, and we must not forget that the ones who were here from the beginning are an integral part of this nation. Those who chose to come later came because there were opportunities here that contributed to their increased sense of well-being. This activity, in and of itself, is a repetition of thousands of years of progress made by the human family. The Human Mandate: Pursue what one perceives to be opportunities to better one's own circumstance as well as that of their primary and extended family's circumstance. This is not new history.

The United States has been a beacon of light and hope for centuries. In this, we must all take pride. However, the fact that sufficient time and resources were not put into the management of the vast tide of immigrants coming to our shores is unpardonable. The truth belongs to itself. We have known what was occurring and we chose to ignore the consequences. It has only recently been discussed with some measure of alarm. That feeling of alarm received a shot in the arm with the events of 9/11/01. There is a substantial and unacceptable risk inherent in allowing the problem to continue unresolved.

Undocumented and therefore illegal aliens are not in the best interests of any lawful society, especially now with those who wish to do us harm and have the ability to carry out their intentions. Policing a society is difficult enough without the added burden of trying to guess who might be entering the country unannounced with the express desire to create havoc and wreck mayhem.

Recommendations

1. Secure the borders. This can be done with a larger border patrol, civilians as well as federal troops, and with hard and electronic intervention/supervision. That, along with biometric identification of all legal U.S. citizens, would create an acceptable environment. This is a national emergency. Sorting out the long-term mix of sufficient numbers of needed personnel will be done as we make progress in taking care of all of the concomitant problems.

2. *Every* agency, be they local, state, federal, or private, should be charged with the responsibility of assessing the legal status of any person involved in any activity that has brought them to the attention of the authorities. Every agency must share that information with all other appropriate agencies. Any state that refuses should suffer the interruption of federal funds, except for those dedicated to the protection of life as well as the maintenance of essential infrastructure.

3. Create immediate legislation that will require that any (I repeat here *any*) employer must ascertain the legal status of an employee. Fines can be set at commensurate levels to ensure compliance.

4. No child should automatically become a citizen of the United States. Children, for the most part, must be presumed the responsibility of someone/parents. There never has been a state thus far in the history of the world that developed a cohesive, caring, responsible society that expected the state to take care of its personal responsibilities. It also goes without saying that any contemporary society that does not have provisions to take care of its own citizens, with the full range of common changes and natural disasters affecting its members, is not a state. This in no way precludes the international assistance given to those tragic victims of natural

disasters. We all must always be ready to lend a hand.

5. Health care benefits should be the natural right of every member of any given society. To be a member of that society all capable members must make the essential contributions to the support of those health care services. (It must be added that Mexico, as well as other nations, has programs of health care that are provided to all eligible citizens.)

6. Clarify the status of every citizen of this nation. From that assessment, create paths to citizenship that are not automatic and do not favor those who have chosen to disregard the current immigration laws.

7. English should be the official language of the United States of America. We are a nation of immigrants, and yet we all must be informed, responsible citizens capable of participating in a national dialog – anyone with everyone.

Special Note About Mexico–U.S. Relations

Mexico, you have the myth and truth of legend and like us, you cannot gloss over history and shout about truth. You must create opportunities for truth to flourish. The plaque at the foot of Lady Liberty says,

> Give me your tired, your poor,
> your huddled masses yearning to breathe free,
> the wretched refuse of your teeming shore.
> Send these, the homeless, tempest-tossed, to me:
> I lift my lamp beside the golden door.

We meant it then and we still mean it, yet we know there must be continuing cohesion to a country and to a culture.

"Come and be recognized!" bespeaks a culture that governs, a country ruled by a deep respect for the rule of law. If we choose to disregard the hard-won order of the ages, we will abandon that fundamental respect for an appreciation of basic human rights – those inherent rights are the foundation of mutual respect for legislation that honors those rights.

To build a wall says we have all failed. How historically idiotic and wasteful is a wall of some 2,000 miles between two neighboring countries in the 21st century?

You have failed in your country to recognize the need for a rule of enforceable laws that are not ignored by an endemic corruption – which is one of the motivating reasons many of you come to a country that is not endemically corrupt.

We have failed in our commitment to uphold those laws and the order that follows from law.

A democratic republic demands an enlightened populace. We have chosen to ignore that responsibility. That this has gone on for such a long time is a sign of the disconnect within a democracy that guarantees freedoms that require a participation in an interdependent quadripartite: an executive, a legislative, a judicial, and an electorate. Only in a continuing vigilance does a democracy flourish.

What is needed from both of our countries is a mutual maturity, one that commits to a growing awareness of, and a responsibility for, the creation of infrastructures that enforce the laws of the land.

Neighbors cannot live with resentments and fear, nor can they be affected by an allegiance to an economics of convenience that, in a fundamental lapse into adolescence, sees only convenience.

This all must be understood in the current environment of a madness that seeks to destroy, to kill and maim. Fundamental methods of protection that provide information essential to safety and order are now a reality. We live in an organic world. Movement occurs, and the challenge for all is to mature in ways that recognize that certain elements must be identified and culled from the civilizations of the 21st century. This will require new modes of life recognition that are in the best interests of all.

Conclusion

Recognizing this natural aspect of human life does not preclude any society from managing the identification of its citizens. I am fully aware that this will place a burden on all members of the society as well as the resources of that society. We must strengthen our resolve and our commitment. The fact that there has been such a broad diversity of penetration into the United States society/economy by illegal aliens helps to ensure that the burden of problem resolution will be shared by the entire society. If any segment is unduly burdened, we can make appropriate adjustments. We must all be aware that there is now a new set of circumstances that warrants the assumption of new responsibilities.

A nation's character is writ largely by the responsibilities that are recognized and met by the citizenry of that nation. The well-being of any group of people, nations included, is a measure of the commitments made by members of that group to its social fabric, meaning to itself and to others. Common cause is one of the cohesive factors in the strengthening of any society. The human society at home and at large is both our individual and communal responsibility. If fundamental communal as well as fundamental individual responsibilities are abrogated and left to states, or nations, the life of that state or nation will be short lived.

NOTE: This 80%, plus or minus, of the human species is of sufficient critical mass to generate a flow of human life from child, to adolescent, to maturing young adult, to maturing adult that can sustain itself. By this I mean that humanity can then spend sufficient time and resources in taking care of, maintaining, and improving the human and environmental conditions without having to spend inordinate resources policing the social whole and reconstructing the infrastructure necessary to allow the human species to continue to grow and develop its full potential. The species becomes synergistically positive and not synergistically negative. In today's world, it actually is quite easy to identify those groups of individuals who, because of an error of perspective, operate with a negative synergism. Venn diagrams would actually allow you to see the countervailing strengths of each group. The overlap of the interface is always in favor of that which enables the whole (critical mass) to grow and to flourish.

You may also wish to see "The Twenty-First Century" in *Murmurings,* along with "Reap the Wind," "Polis Mundi," "Refugees," "Transmigration," "Who Is My Brother and My Sister?," and for those Mexicans recently arrived, or for those still at home, "And the Soul?" in *Always Extolling.*

IRAQ – THE LAST WAR

As we attempt to gain a deeper understanding of the current global circumstance, especially with reference to war, we may now have sufficient data to say, "Iraq should be "THE LAST WAR."

This does not mean that conflicts and conflict resolution is a thing of the past. It simply means that war as we have come to know it should be gone from the world stage. This is not to say that there won't be resolutions and embargoes, all of which must have deadlines and the willingness to address and redress. In order to accomplish all this there must also be a communal commitment to "surgical interventions" as a working tool of humanity.

The UN is ill equipped to do this at the present time and for the foreseeable future. This must not deter any nation, or group of nations, from taking on this responsibility. The global stage is beset with humanitarian crises of great proportions, most of which are of a political nature. Not all member nations are disposed to share in this responsibility at this moment in time. However, those that are should be willing to share proportionately in a measure of that responsibility by assuming their share of participation in these surgical interventions – whether as part of the Strike Force, in a support role, or later as stability maintenance, and development. The objectives of interventions should be to establish a rule of law, law that punishes anyone who chooses to operate outside the International Bill of Human Rights.

War

The conditions that prevailed throughout human history that lead to war are waning. We are now being presented with a new critical mass of developments that can end the perpetuation of history's warring efforts as we have come to know them. We will not be free of skirmishes, vendettas, armed insurrections and the like, including riots. Indeed, the acceleration of the implosion of humanity will not stop. Heat will rise and there will be friction. However, the warring techniques that destroy whole infrastructures of a people will no longer be tolerated for any length of time from the inside or from the outside of any country. This does not mean that we will (ever) be without those who choose to disrupt any circumstance. However, they will not matter when it comes to the movement of the whole. There are at hand methodologies and a developing focus, be they imperfect, for dealing with them as a part of the whole.

The global economic infrastructure binds us in ways that ripple instantly in ever-increasing magnitudes. The meta-levels of these globally supportive infrastructures, those necessary to foster and maintain a cohesive, productive global whole, are such that the current understanding by most nations penetrates the whole. This will promote behavior that, although still wrought with a level of violence towards members of our own kind, does not carry sufficient weight to forestall interaction, or to destroy us all.

The new truth seems to be that a large subjugated population maintaining a fidelity to a fear-driven perspective cannot exist for long, given the current status of technology and information. This situation will preclude any lengthy warring effort. Even seemingly benevolent dictators will be condemned to short tenure. All things move and we move according to our own kind in our own time. We are a freedom-seeking species, self-coincidental beings busy becoming that which we already are, mitigated only by our ability to choose in order to continue to be what we are, believe that we are, and can become. This fact, along with the historical fact that most of us will not choose to self-destruct, or destroy in an ever-increasing fashion, means that (for the foreseeable future) there will be many more of us living with each other, with more of what we create for each other and acquire from each other.

This dynamic interchange will provide new opportunities for all members of the human family to participate in the creative potential of the species. A warning to the dotcoms and multinationals, as well as those whose avarice has yet to be owned: there will be a concerted effort on the part of any intervening coalition to put everyone at the disposition of courts of law. Any lawlessness, along with price inflation, gauging, and monopolistic forms of control will not be permitted.

If the aforementioned circumstances possess a sufficient amount of transparency – that is, information permeates the whole very quickly (the evidence that this is happening is overwhelming) – it makes clear that we need to commit to a fidelity of a progressively assertive posture. In order for us to maintain this assertive stance with "organic integrity" (applicable to us all in a timely fashion), it would be helpful for us to have a definition of being that "cradles" us as well as "throws" us ahead. Notwithstanding the social and economic dislocations brought about by interventions, attempts must be made to establish and maintain communication as well as infrastructures that provide any group of people access to sufficient resources and opportunities to continue with their pursuits of life.

Aristotle's observation that "people will not remain idle" augurs well for an acceptance of the laws of physics as they pertain to human behavior. Bodies in motion stay in motion – tending to some form of curvature – putting them in different space over time. The case is being made that we are too occupied, as a species, to interrupt our current involvement for long periods of time to needlessly destroy others, or infrastructures that have taken so long to build and maintain, precisely because they meet a growing, human need. The biology of the moment also presents us with sufficient information to allow for a position-taking that has integrity as a fundamental point of departure. This means that we cannot ensconce ourselves in a punctilious adolescence that denies, or negates, the obvious. This "new integrity" must be based on an organic reality that is always "flowing," or "jumping," and yet remaining "close enough" to what is already there.

A note for those so occupied with the numbers of dead presented as daily fare – they too were always there – and we cannot allow the omnipresent media to distract us from our universal commitments and the facts of our everyday lives. That would truly be a tragedy, leading inevitably to greater numbers of dead. This does not mean that we can choose to disregard the indiscriminant loss of life and the subsequent tragedy that befalls all of us. We all need to respond swiftly to any and all circumstances that need attention. This must be done lest we condemn ourselves to live with memories connected to voids where previously there were others of our kind.

A New Point of Beginning

We must accept a perspective on life that disposes all of us to move towards what is perceived as *really right*, an honest, reflected-upon, integrated perception of reality. In this knowing moment, really knowing with further reflection, when we still appear to be moving along our "human curve" with a comfort zone that allows us to stay focused on humanity's goals, we sense a premonition, coming from a point of departure that is *close enough* to the truth, and we choose to act for the common good. All of this means that we are responsible for what we know now. Ownership of truth that is *close enough* in the now has always been being's existential mandate.

Perhaps a working definition of humanity will be of some assistance. If being human (at our "close enough" actual level) is *being a rational social animal, a fabricator, a destroyer,* [*] *a symbolizing, freedom-seeking, soul-pondering, sentient being*, then each and every one of us needs to be about this from the center of our own being. History has demonstrated that this is, indeed, what most of us have been about for some time. Current reality continues to confirm this.

The palaver of the "right" and of the "left," the warring dispositions of the "haves" and "have-nots," or those in the arenas of Utopian or Tragic visions notwithstanding, must eventually succumb to an understanding of an organic reality. This would have from its "center" a rational core that accommodates the concepts of healthy and sick, bound and directed particles, as well as "free" radicals. If nature has "done well" with its historical and current circumstance it will be difficult for us to do less.

Therefore, … in this moment of global opportunity we should all be about living with the utmost integrity, being what we already are and sharing what we already are with each other in

---

[*] See note on page 42.

some form of paced activity that happens in human time. This includes the willingness to educate continuously, provide resources where and when they are needed, medicate when necessary, and excise cancers using a variety of techniques when they threaten the individual and corporate health of the species.

NOTE: A lengthy discussion is not necessary to conclude that a given part of humanity is destructive. The percentage of most populations possessing this trait has historically been relatively small; consequently their impact, for the most part, has been small. Technology will continue to magnify their impact potential and therefore an "eternal vigilance" will always be in order. You may wish to peruse *The Anatomy of Human Destructiveness* (Erich Fromm) and *The Game of Life: A Player's Manual for Executives and Others*, as well as "Messages" from *The Swamps of Time* and "Fields of Sacrifice" and "Conspiracy" from *Always Extolling* (by Don Davison).

SELF-LOVE[*]

We can all relate to our past – the journey we embarked upon called life. All of us come into life for the first time and we struggle to get some sort of understanding about the world and ourselves. Sometimes we do not get started quite right. How much is too much? How much is too little? These are not questions we can answer as a child. It is only with great difficulty that we attempt some answers as adults. Only when we are on the road to maturity can we ever hope to gain a measure of understanding that will enable us to know, somewhat, how much is too much and how much is too little. We learn in the eternal movement of life that perhaps living is a matter of coming "close enough."

The question of having enough love has crossed all of our minds at some point in the life journey. However, for the most part, in the reflective recesses of our human hearts, we wonder only intermittently if we have enough self-love. Yet it is only when we cross this threshold of self-love that we begin to understand what it is to have enough of this precious commodity; only then can we really begin to relate in some honest fashion to the rest of creation and ourselves.

Self-love demands an honesty that separates us from everything else into everything else. We are born into the arms of life and we die into the arms of the All. The only thing that we

---

[*] For an in-depth discussion of self-love see *The Game of Life: A Player's Manual for Executives and Others.*

can honestly do from birth to death is to share ourselves with ourselves and with others. In order to do this sharing it is essential that we know ourselves, who we really are, and then care enough to interact honestly with our surrounds, respecting in both what is eternally already there. This is what we already know ourselves to be, and in making heroic choices, choose to become. Finally, in that supreme act of self-ownership, we exude a personal responsibility, and live for all that we are.

What is it that we share? In *The Art of Loving*, Eric Fromm tells us that it is "time being." This is our time, a limited, brief, passing moment, this is all that we have and all that we can share.

What is this "time being" that we must share and how must we share ourselves? What we share must be something very real. If we were to share anything else, the not real, we would waste our being in time and the time being of any other. Therefore, the most precious thing is truth itself, which must be shared with self and all others in order to be efficient with the laws of nature and of God.

If we lie, about anything, we lose, and those around us also lose. It is also imperative that we know that a lie of any kind is first to self and then to others. We must also remember that lies can be of two kinds: omission and commission. Adolescents are masters of the lie of omission. Many believe that only in this halo of silence can they find themselves and nurture sufficient strength to withstand the pressures of both the inside and outside of reality.[*] The greater truth is that it is only with the birth of self-love that we come to know that it is in sharing love

---

[*] See "What Is That?" in *Iris and Other Things.*

that we grow.[**] We must also know that truth can exist independent of our knowledge of it. We can therefore omit that which is true and that which we do not know, or we can choose to distort reality and "bend" what we share to some different perspective. When this is intentional, we become as tinkling cymbols, or sounding brass. We are out of sync with the orchestra of the world/universe.

We could get lost in intellectual debate about the fact that anything we create must in some way be a reflection of the Divine, and therefore we are exonerated from any and all responsibility to coincide with any truth, other than that which just is, whether it is our creation or not. The Truth, however, can have a life of its own and our challenge is to coincide with it when we become aware of it, precisely because it is already there. The worst form of dishonesty is to wait when we know the truth. The truth commands. Our challenge is to obey, to own the truth as soon as we know it. The present is always our most fertile playing field.

We are all aware of things that we say or do that lack integrity. Our never-ending challenge must be to recognize that whatever truth there is, is already there, somewhere. There must be some reality, or piece of reality, that possesses the Truth that we can coincide with, be one with. How foolish we are when it comes to exercising our own responsibility. We cannot escape ourselves. We already are what we are as we emerge into life, and we self-define in some incredibly individual fashion as we mature and coincide with what we "really" know.

The Truth is there in a form of being that has a focused attribute that manifests itself in the following manner: when

---

[**] See "Sharing" in *Murmurings.*

you know com-passion (a loving awareness of self and other), there is a wisdom that does not interdict in the process of life – it complements life. This means there is a deep respect for others and a silent strength in their presence that gives you and them the freedom to be who you and they really are. This synergism is a complementary form of symbiosis, a pattern of the organic that belongs to the species/universe. We are seeing this in the newfound freedoms of democracy as they spread throughout the world.

We would not be hard pressed to cite examples of commitments that cost us time and energy, suppressing an awareness of the sanctity of our own life and of all life. It has taken the species so much time to get to know itself and consequently to recognize self in others, all others.

The greatest expression of our self-love is in knowing ourselves, in owning our own truth as a caring, responsible, and respecting entity, while always expressing ourselves with a fundamental integrity that is clear to all.

Topics for further discussion:

Understanding the postmodern disorganization of the reorganization
The display
Adolescent ravings and machinations that belie the value of commitments and friendships as it pertains to the greater truths (virtues) of any project or *purpose of being*
The turning

How do we recognize sufficient numbers of individuals who emerge from the personhood of their time and accept the eternal gauntlet of Knighthood and Ladyship, those that can stand on the horizon of changing times holding their shields of love and waving their swords of truth in mighty gestures towards those who deny the embodiment of beauty and eternal truths?

To exude a commitment to the importance of each individual in the imploding present is of paramount importance. Corporations (multinational and otherwise) of our time must exude an integrity of purpose in every endeavor: in personnel, management, R&D, production, transportation, marketing, and capital derivation, and ROI (return on investment).

We must all acknowledge and remember that every wandering and wondering soul needs guideposts and leaders that can help them know that they are on the right path in embracing their humanity by the confirmation of their own being as it relates to all being.[*]

---

[*] See "Reap the Wind" and "Touching" in *Always Extolling.*

THANK YOU, ARTISTS!

There is a need to pay closer attention to the artists of every pursuit, those creative geniuses who specialize in reading the waves of human emotions and comprehensions by conveying and displaying them. By sifting and winnowing gems of perception and fathoming the leading edges of humanity's sensitivities, they bear witness for us all. They are the capturers of those scintillating depths of feelings that give us glimpses of greater and deeper truths – truths that flame images into blinded eyes and send messages into deafened ears – truths that will create new history – truths that chart new courses for the ship of human life.

How can we apprehend those glimpses of truths and fantasy? How difficult to tell the chaff from the kernels. It all starts as a child's mind might reflect, might wonder. "Which one is it? What are they?" At an early age, we are taught our numbers – addition and subtraction and those dreaded fractions. So what are the common denominators found among the great truths and what is the extent of the human imagination? Where are those connectors that bring integration to an understanding of it all? We know they must be there, or they, those stalwart enemies and allies – our teachers – would not be asking us to find them. We learn early on that if they ask for answers, they ought to be there somewhere. So what are those common denominators, those that really fit the grand human template?

It is to the arts that we look and seek after the enjoyment and awe of finding the hominid's place in the grand scheme. It is where the sought-after that fits the common denominators of us all are lying. It is there where those brilliant shafts of light, of understanding, bathe life with more life and bring a readiness to touch things and others in ways that brings the warmth of common being to any interchange.

Today it is not a number, although numbers play a part in some of the formulaic production – it is now our common ground that seeks fertilization, seeks to bear the fruits of appreciation and understanding. In our search for answers, answers that are the common denominators of the species, this we know: for the most part, they are not a common language, or common religion, or common politic. They run much deeper. They also seem to come at inopportune moments.

Take courage, you artists of the ages – lay out your wares with bold aplomb and move on to greater depths of expression. Many of you come as unpopular guests, even heretics to the party of life. Yet you artists, ever faithful to your visions, present your fare! Stay your course when the frail edges of our current perception of reality are not sufficient for your given purpose.

Meanwhile, we, the rest of us in our biased turpitude, are basking in less-than-eager form where sloth of purpose binds our souls. We must all get closer to the core, closer to the heart. The values we must seek are terminal values connecting human matter, mitochondrial truths that form a cross-stitch holding the Holy for us all. Life belongs to life, mine to yours and yours to mine. The insignificant does not hold the truth – it merely colors it. Yet, like fundamental condiments, salt and pepper, we too belong to the tree of life. Indeed, we are branches of that tree. We owe our being to the trunk and always to the new shoots, shoots that become leading edges, the children of us all. It is here that the artist's template wrought from eternal fire must effervesce in the sea of possibilities.

We must acknowledge this greater truth, we must bear witness to its fundamental reality. We must be ecumenical in our understanding. Complementing life is what we are all about. We must also bear the brunt of those whose values are of insufficient quality to add new foliage. It is not easy to hold at bay the madness of extraneous malevolence, yet we must stand still in silent awe, and then sing in the unison of commitment, "Yes to life!"

Praise to all those parents who teach their offspring the depths of the meaning of knowledge, care, responsibility, and respect; these are the eternal common denominators for all life. For it is with these that we will find what we all must have, and it is with these that we will construct our paths to paradise.

THE MEDIATION OF REALITY

The evolutionary process has provided the stage upon which life has been exposed to an omnipresence that on the one hand has been benevolent and on the other hand unforgiving. The mandate *pay attention or die!* has always been the key for success in life's efforts.

The advent of mediation that emanates outside the person has always provided an opportunity for the species to adapt and complement personal and communal existence. The inclusion of information accumulated over time in our species' world view has created the various cultural points of departure. Some are more compatible with life than others. Some of this information not only became the artifacts of the ages, it also became part of a fundamental genetic code that perpetuates itself as an "open" opportunity for survival. It still labors in this task.

In the course of events, events that for us were initially paced by our own being, we interfaced with the forces of nature and others of our own kind. Along the way, there were interludes that provided for reflective repose, opportunities to integrate a deeper measure of understanding, ultimately leading to different levels of freedom. This freedom, in turn, gave us greater opportunity to create.

In our current moment, we have harnessed a considerable inventory of energy forms that present us with new challenges. We are now opting to mediate our existence with the seemingly ever-present power of electricity. As the aftermath of some of the great storms of recent history so aptly have demonstrated, electricity is a provisional form of energy that in its many applications can provide for amenities that enhance human life while creating a definitive dependence that inhibits in some ways the use of our senses, which then places us at some measure of risk.

One of electricity's gifts has been the ubiquitous television. It has provided us with a vast host of opportunities that, while providing us with seemingly impossible audio-visual exposures, has also given us the opportunity to experience, albeit from a distance, myriad pieces of information. In saying this, we know that if information is in any form, it is in some sense "real." We also know that some of the effects of electronic games / simulations can provide an edge to winning and perhaps even survival. Having noted this, we nevertheless would still like to point out that the monitor (what a word that is!) does not replace the warmth of another person. There is no substitute for a live presence. Ask the infirm, the shut-ins. A computer or TV offers scant solace compared to the presence of a friend.

There is no doubt that the presentation of information, especially in the new age of electronically generated and enhanced sounds as well as computer-generated graphics, has blurred the lines of reality. This blurring can have the net effect of compromising our ability to reason out the most fruitful opportunities that present themselves and that could be inculcated into our current and future worldview, opportunities that may complement our quality of life. We must also remember that the world cannot "really be seen" from a couch or armchair. It smells, tastes, and generates feelings that feed us from a different plate – a plate that makes for a substantially healthier meal.

Although history has given us ample evidence that all new creations burst forth with a plethora of applications, some of which have questionable value, we are still in many cases preoccupied with merely childlike applications of some forms of technology. I say this knowing that a form of childishness is essential in the creative and integrative process. Yet in many areas of technological application, we still seem to be in an adolescent stage with our development of appropriate uses of these new technologies. Our penchant for creation must be tempered by our willingness to adopt a maturing responsibility. One can argue that the intent of the vast majority of our creations was stimulated by some felt need to make something fit, to work, or to play, ostensibly to better the human condition, indeed the conditions of all life. Nevertheless, the famous and infamous *Law of Unintended Consequences* continues to haunt us and to surprise us with its ever-present menu of the good and the bad. The good may be placed at the disposal of the malevolent and the bad may become an essential complement to a newly discovered set of needy circumstances. It is in our seasoning and maturing that we ultimately fathom the difference.

As the plethora of technology continues to burst across the globe, our current understanding needs a more reasoned and compassionate approach. One of the mitigating factors in gaining access to this understanding is (still) the omnipresence of television and the way it is utilized.

Much of what is currently being produced by the media of television incorporates an inordinate mix of applications. In addition, we would say there is an inherent value to an eclectic approach, one that follows nature's hidden path. However, we would also say that if we could mirror nature's efficient abundance, an abundance that does not place the balance too far from the center, we would be following an efficaciously well-worn path.

On our current trail, we provide too few turnouts for repose. This continuing penchant for excess, for the most part, has less than a salutary effect on the species' ability to parse out needed from confusing and gratuitous information. Nowhere is this more evident than in the programs that we have come to regard as essential to the very survival of the species. News, or euphemistically Current Events, or of the current moment – "Happening Now!" – is now more than ever presented as docudrama, or infotainment, and now quite dishonestly as a Commentary.

To have the current level of omnipresence of the "on" television in our daily lives bespeaks a certain lack of understanding about our historically beneficial pastimes of seeking a stillness that provides reflective repose, a repose that is so essential in sorting the real truths from waves and waves of information, or what now has become "Data Smog."[*]

The screens of current television production are bathed in a superabundance of interdictory and contradictory facts, figures, flashes, movements, and circumstances that can only be sorted out by those with sufficient experience and/or ability to withstand an increasingly high rate of what is now being understood to be an artificial comprehension. It has been questioned for some time whether this is in the best interests of the species. Thinking that we know is certainly different from understanding what we know.

---

[*] David Shenk.

We must also be aware that what is news for one is not news for the other. Yes, we understand that different venues can complement different subject matter. However, we are also familiar with the arguments that advocate for the need to have some species-wide understanding. It can also be said that there will be no such understanding without an individual ownership of presence to give it meaning. Please be aware that there is some communal responsibility connected to all of this. We must also add that individual presence, in order to be efficiently committed to its personal and social well-being, must be operating with a measure of personal integrity that many times trumps any other piece of information. The journey of biology is very personal and is always with us.

Having said all of this, it seems there is a need for an in-depth understanding of an individual and corporate humanity that struggles with the difficulties of survival as it sorts out its consumptive habits. Given the current state of global implosion, it would seem that this individual and communal understanding must be of paramount importance. This being the case, there is a need for an enlightened approach to presenting information that has, ostensibly, some measure of universal importance for the survival of the species.

Please be a little magnanimous and do not be offended by this "simple focus." We also understand that there is a need for contemplation and for entertainment.

We also fully understand that while there is a lecture on the absolute need to maintain clean water taking place at some international forum, there may be some catastrophe occurring in some other part of the planet. The challenge is, and has always been, to pay attention to our circumstantial now in ways that ensure and optimize our ability to incorporate information that becomes part of our survival tool chest. We will always need those other goodies to assist those around us with their survival.

This brings us to our current manifold menus of the news. A screen display that presents up to six venues (and now sometimes more – I wrote this yesterday!) for the viewer to comprehend is not offering sufficient space/time to sort out what is essential to its current audience. The challenge currently facing the many attempts to inform the local and global constituency is to maintain a commitment to essential information and to shy away from a form of questionable recreation called infotainment. There is time for this and that, it does not have to be all of one color! Viewers are cheated on the information side of the platform and assaulted on the other with excess that attempts to entertain.

The wisdom of the ages is clear – there can be an inherent enjoyment in the acquisition of information that is in our best interest.

Smoke, fire, screeching tires, broken glass, bloodletting, shouting, screaming, hurling of obscenities, pornography, and the various diatribes of madness are not the only stimulating forms of presentation. When the catastrophic does occur, a flashing from scene to scene does not provide the same degree of comprehension as reflective repose that feeds our awe and elicits a response. We must have interludes to allow for a sinking in of the magnitude of the event. It must be added that essential decorum in the "talk shows" (this is now rapidly becoming an oxymoron) needs to be maintained for the benefit of everyone. The current abundance of shouting matches belittles us as participants and sends all too corrosive messages to our children.

The degree to which a news organization is able to serve local and global ends can be measured in its ability to sort out the essential and present it in such a way that sufficient repose is incorporated in the presentation. Enlightenment is the goal. It must also be noted that taste mirrors a culture's ability to recognize that what we do is ultimately and always done for the young. To pursue an eternal elevation of our understanding must be our most human pastime.

THE PAST – THE PRESENT – THE FUTURE

The closeness of another of our kind – not one, or two, or three, but many – seems to have shaken our inner equilibrium. While trying to stay connected to the "out there" and the "in here" of human existence, we are now taxing our instinctual and rational wherewithal beyond its current ability to synthesize an understanding of real meaning. We are being swept into the pace of the day. Many now wander lost in a paradise of pilled pleasures and entertainment ad nauseam, wracked with anxiety and shrouded in a cloud of doom. Only intermittent glimpses of light beckon them towards new horizons.

The miracle in all of this is that these intermittent flashes give birth to a never-dying hope. To every time, there are those cloudy days, those cold nights. Still, from the depths of despair and agony, the human spirit rises from its knees and steps forward in its own time. May we never forget the necessary effort that precedes accomplishment and may we, from the depths of our being, draw forth sufficient strength of purpose doing what we know how to do with sufficient integrity to share what we believe is right with those we love.

Some measure of context and understanding is essential in taking and maintaining a "stand point" in comprehending and interfacing with "reality." It demands our reasoned and careful participation. What deserves our effort? What truly matters to the well-being of the species? Where does the bridge between life and death lead us? What matters enough for us to choose to be heroic in the face of the madnesses of an age?

61

Some Context

Historically the "out there" was of vital concern. There were those entities and conditions that were most perilous for the upright ape, the humanizing anthropoid. "Pay attention!" was the gift of our long trial of instinctual awareness as small groups of us wandered the hidden and open spaces of our given environs. As the "in here" began to boil, to percolate, shadows of our awareness – gifts of the complexity of our growing neocortex – created tensions that came to play with still more "others," and along with those similar others our creations of culture, language, tools, and toys gave us edges that were advantages and disadvantages in life's great epic journey.

The sorting out of the shadows, the growth of the internal infrastructure, along with an imagination, challenged us to fathom essential connections of the life-affirming kind and those of a destructive ilk. Some forty thousand years on, we still labor at the task. Not because there are the same dangers from meat-eating predators, but because we have continued to imagine and the environment has continued to give us omnipresent "others": climate, natural disasters, disease, an onslaught of "creations," and many more others of our kind.

What would it be like to throw something very fast, very far, and very hard? What would it be like to have a closed-in, hard-walled dwelling? What would it be like to tame the bull and ride the horse? What would happen if we planted seeds and waited throughout the seasons? What would it be like to fly? What would it be like to stop pain? What would it be like to know medicine? What does spirituality really mean? We have wondered and we have created. In addition, as we created, we fathomed ways to harness more and more of Nature's hidden potentials.

Some Understanding

We have "created" electricity, "split" the atom, "discovered" penicillin, and "divined" countless cures and palliatives. Now we visit a space station as well as send our eyes and ears into the heavens to assist our earthbound ponderings about the "way out there," the beginning, the journey, or the final destination of it all. While we continue on our way, basking in the comfort of our new surroundings, warm shelters and fields laden with food, we have learned to use the electron to share ideas in audio, written, and picture form. In the interim, our inherited instincts became, or so some have been lulled into thinking, less efficient, less essential.

The greater truth is that unless we operate from an ever-increasing synthesized and integrated perspective of the whole, we do so at tremendous risk to self and others. We need only to look at the poor, the destitute, the maligned, the starving, to know that we need to increase our awareness and our under-standing of what it means to be a brother and a sister to all our brothers and sisters. Some are older, some are younger, some have too much, some too little, and some have very different beliefs.

Now, when those few of us so inclined choose to ponder the happenings of our days and the depths of the meaning of existence, as we continue to fathom the whys and what fors of our interface with the "out there" and the "in here," some of our attempts seem to have been both sublime and ridiculous. We have even succumbed to the worshiping of both. Yet the truth lies in our relationship to ourselves and to others. We must live embodying an unfinished reciprocity that commands and is always "there" or "here." Hegel's/Heidegger's Dasein is always intended movement.[*] Currently, we seem to have difficulty focusing in our moment with a universal caring that holds life as sacred and therefore deserving of our most revered commitment to follow Nature's path.

The present bears witness to our depths of understanding (and lack thereof) and our creative genius (and madness of our creations). We still wonder who and what our enemy is, as well as wondering about our neighbors, the "different" ones, errant asteroids, a tiny virus, cancers, or in some elevated and honest reflection, our lack of integrity when it comes to caring for ourselves and others of our own kind, or our ecological environs.

A dichotomy has arisen from our accumulated contemplations of our ability to get along with our current social circumstances. What was once considered a synthesizing relative benevolence appears now to be perhaps malevolent encounters, a clash of civilizations. Minds, mad and otherwise, have come to believe that in death, we bequeath serenity and health to ourselves and to the living, and that this can be true and not true. Too many of us are preoccupied with "products" from the consumption industries. We wallow in a stupor, smiling and shouting at each other, secure in our shared narcoticized state that everyone is doing it (whatever it is) therefore it must be right, it must be true; it must be what we all need/want. In that encapsulation of need and want, we stumble and fall from our pedestals of enlightenment and rush with the maddening crowds toward the unfulfilled of the less-thans and the have-nots of our media-saturated imaginations. Stop! Salvation lies in that ancient awareness: enough is enough, when true (really honestly true), then true.

---

[*] Da-sein is Hegel's and Heidegger's term. It is that omnipresent intentionality of being-ness that we all are a part of, and that we can choose to know.

Only in prayerful repose, focused on existing truths – truths leading to more truths (life itself) – can we ever hope to fathom our next step. Notwithstanding the heroics of the ages – why do we insist on a failure of understanding that in the realm of life enough is a moving state of being, a maintenance of what has come to be and is now already here? So many people continue to utilize time and energy (their time-being), sloshing through the swamps of less than, of base unbecoming behavior, or rabid senseless screaming matches that neither enlighten nor elevate our understanding. Why does the secular's mundaneness capture and hold fast to a part of all of this? Has that elf, gnome, fairy, or whatever of our curiosity (the other side of our imagination), now lost its sense of justness, of grace, or, or ... does it all matter enough to have a meaning for all of those who need our protection and our nurturing?

A Conclusion

We have before us a holy choice: Choose to care honestly enough for self so that you can choose to honestly care enough for another. We need to choose to want to know what enough is as the ever-growing depths of truths are unveiled. We must also exercise our responsibility to ourselves and our circumstances with a complementing integrity that is extended to all others in the sacred crucible of time.

Looking into the bright and clear eyes of our children, indeed all children, we must ask ourselves, what will become of them? Will they honor the gods of our ancestors, those that honored life? Will they come to know that life can only be an act of redemption leading to salvation if we come to know and to understand the sacredness of it all? And finally, can they come to know this if we do not show them the way?

THE PERSON

```
                *
              *   *
            *   *   *
          *  PSYCHO  *
        *  *  *  *  *  *  *
  * Birth *   * THE HUMAN UNIT *    * Death *
        *  *  *  *  *  *  *
          * CHEMICAL *
            *   *   *
              *   *
                *
```

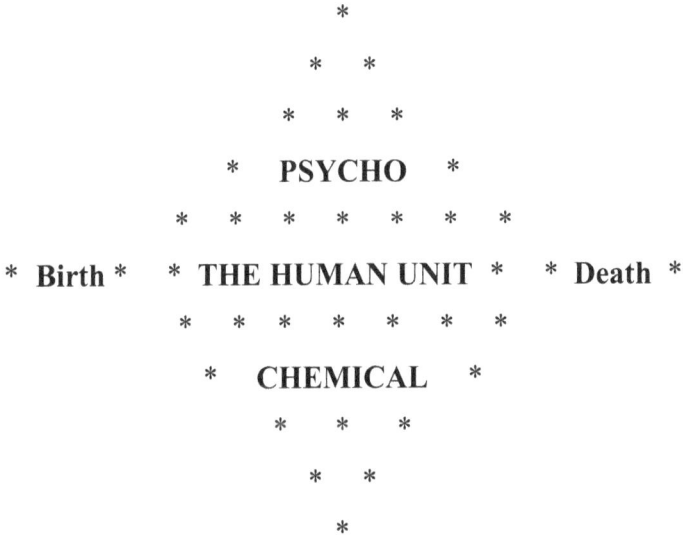

The "human unit" is a psychochemical phenomenon that emerges at birth and leaves this mortal coil at death. To be a person one must accept the relationship between two inter-facing realities. We are psychochemical units inextricably linked. We are body and soul, as the ancients put it, or mind and body, as the moderns express it. In addition to atoms and molecules, we are something else; we know that we exist and we relate to others. This relationship makes the human experience a heroic exercise. Decisions, commitments, and choices must be made to maintain a faithful focus of purpose. The journey through changing events and the seasons of our time has all of the necessary ingredients for a true adventure.

The continuing wealth of information concerning our well-being encompasses every field of knowledge. The dawning of the 21st century brings with it the vast storehouse of the accumulated wisdom of the species, and our challenge is to use everything at our disposal in a timely fashion in order to live creatively and productively.

Any number of studies have concluded that a measure of our current absence of well-being as a species is generated not only by a lack of understanding of what the "human road" is all about, but also by a lack of the integration of our human attributes as we interface with a world beset with communication that sets up psychosomatic conditioning. The following pages will attempt to shed some light on this state of affairs and will use as a point of departure a model that is cognitive, emotional, and physical (organic). To round out a person's growth we will also be pointing out the need for a personal and communal as well as spiritual commitment.

As the "rational social animal," we have developed and left for posterity examples of our commitment to a spiritual reality. Archeological evidence of this abounds. History is evidence that we have tried to care for each other in this life, and standing in awe about the Great Beyond, have sent many on their journey to the "unknown" with the necessary tools, food, and other amenities. We have, as well, acknowledged something called "grace" – a state of being that somehow prepares us for and allows us to participate well in our current life and in some hereafter.

Personal and communal ceremonies have always been a part of being a person among others. The individual commitment and the communal participation have served to exercise our involvement in the process of being. This involvement has been as a particular event, living our own lives, while we interface in a universal event, a society of others, and the world/universe. This interplay between self and others as an expression of our physical, intellectual, emotional, and spiritual presence in the process of life, is essential in defining human reality.

As we move deeper into the 21st century, we are becoming aware of our personal and communal participation in a global family of events, encompassing more than just the human, and essential to the whole earth. In stepping into this new knowledge about the interdependency of all being, we must maintain a fidelity to ourselves as responsible beings, aware of self and circumstance. This we will discuss later in some detail. For now, engrossed as we are in our concern for personal and global well-being, let us begin by looking at what this thing called "person" really is.

The following diagram will help us set the stage for an understanding of the four attributes of the person: intellectual, emotional, physical, and spiritual. We will use a simple stick figure to represent the player of The Game of Life. Each player can flesh out their individuality as a person and weave their own multicolored fabric for their personhood as they learn to play.

If a person feels happy and healthy, they probably are. However, with our current level of understanding of biology, we must maintain an enlightened vigilance against those insidious silent states of creeping physical diseases such as cancers and heart disease. We must schedule appropriate preventive physical assessments as a matter of balanced health maintenance, while developing and maintaining an appropriately balanced regimen of intellectual, emotional, and spiritual well-being that season with us.

* * *

Review the Diagram of Person on Page 35 of *The Game of Life*.[*]

(See a brief synopsis below.)

[The diagram of a stick figure on page 35 of *The Game of Life* indicates the four theaters of human operation and their inherent and potential attributes: (1) The Intellectual with *capacity and history*, (2) The Emotional with *predisposition and disposition*, (3) The Physical with *innate and developmental*, and (4) The Spiritual with *history and capacity*.]

Note that there is a movement from the heart through the brain that has a holistic comprehension that not only "owns the whole person," but also "connects" the person to the whole. Current research is looking at the electromagnetic Taurus that is emitted from the heart. It has even been called the fourth brain. Indeed, in today's world we seem to be thresholding on a deeper understanding of the feminine – that is, women "think" with their hearts much more than men do, and with both sides of their brain at once. They involve their whole body in their reality interface. This can set up a complementary synergism that maximizes the human potential. The masculine and feminine need each other.

* * *

---

[*] This section, "The Person," is an excerpt from *The Game of Life: A Manual for Executives and Others*.

70

The interplay and balance between the attributes of the intellectual, emotional, physical, and spiritual, along with their subsequent characteristics, make up what we shall call Personhood. Personhood is something that we are born with and yet must learn to wear and continue to grow into as we mature through life's seasons. If we size our Personhood to the Truth of Self in the Now, it fits and we become maturing, balanced, productive individuals who are able to reap the benefits of a dynamic and happy life. If, on the other hand, we never learn to put on our Personhood, we maintain dysfunctional coping mechanisms that inhibit our freedom and development, and we never attain that full measure of happiness that should be the goal and right of every person.

In today's world, for many people (we recognize the inhibiting effects of war, natural disasters, and underdeveloped infrastructures) there is increasingly an unprecedented opportunity to accept responsibility to be all that we are and all that we can be. In order for this to happen, a self-learning profile must be adopted at an early age and a fidelity to personal growth and development must be maintained. This dedication to self-purpose must also be integrated with knowledge of time and place in the world of today. This integrated knowledge of self and circumstance brings with it a concomitant responsibility to the others within our realm. A necessary understanding of our own species as well as all other species, and of physical reality, is indispensable. We are part of a whole in which we must participate knowingly and responsibly.

The starting point for this participation is the Self. We must grasp a moving and yet somewhat focused sense of purpose that we can feel is ours, a destiny over which we have some measure of control and yet has of necessity an essential co-participation in a greater being. We are therefore both personally and corporately responsible for the well-being of others and ourselves.

This prevailing circumstance brings to the forefront some essential questions – age-old philosophical questions – that need answers. What is a person? What is real? These fundamental questions have been broadened by information from the fields of paleontology, biology, and astrophysics to a more focused effort that is asking the old questions in a more personal fashion. They have become a quest for self. Who do I think I am? Who do others think I am? Who am I really? Where am I going? How am I going to get there? These questions touch the thread of our historical continuity of a being in time, and they address ethical mandates that have come to have an ever more increasing urgency in the light of the current process of human growth and development.

"Know thyself and to thine own self be true."

"Love thy neighbor as thyself."

There seems to be much in history that tells us what things are or have been; there also seems to be some history that tells us how things were and are. The philosophers have spoken to the issue of Being – what reality is and how the many faces of reality present themselves to us. This we also know; there is much that is not presented to us. Visible and audible reality is just that – visible and audible. The spectrums of particle and wave hint at much more on both ends.

In that great bell curve of our reality – knowing there is something more to "the whole" – our challenge is to live within the now of our personal and corporate circumstance. That the human species – the person – has become the single interdictoriest element in the current global moment is now apparent.

Paleontologists, archaeologists, anthropologists, and historians have hinted to the movement of the wandering anthropoid turned hominid. This movement of our kind has finally netted the globe and the telltale signs of our increasing activity are everywhere.

In this "new era," our current presence has set a course that is now seemingly at odds with the biodiversity of not only our own species, but that of other species as well. Where do we go to find semblances of some Golden Age, an age where things seem to have recognizable values and where the direction of history seems to make sense? There is a need for us now to seek out some profound understanding of our own time that will give us a measure of protection from ourselves and give a protective halo to the process of all life. We look and wait for some quantum leap of understanding that will give rise to a new perception of some new Golden Age, an age that seeks the very best in all things and assumes responsibility for our participation in the great cosmic interplay.

Within the intertwines of the present global economic infrastructure, there is a message: we are proceeding on a course that is consumptive and too destructive, a course that seems to hold some catastrophe as a fixed horizon. Notwithstanding the theological tenets of Faith, Hope, and Charity, there seems to be a need for some commanded integrity that leads us to the Truth of the Now, a truth that gives us an understanding of the reciprocity of the parts to the whole. Is there something that might present an opportunity to heal this wound of our current myopic perspective? Perhaps the thought might be – "growth in time."

What does this growth in time mean? If we could find some icon of being that has meaning for us now that would translate into a position we could take on reality, we could then focus our considerable talents on a formidable response to this "growth in time" with an understanding that meets the mandates of integrity. As we search through the annals of our record in history, the person's presence on land, in the sea, and in the air, there seems to be only two historical images that draw our attention: the shepherd and the fisherman. We have not yet spent enough time in space to garner a meaningful understanding of our presence there, although collisions of our space debris and the aftermath send us warning signals. Of the other two, at this juncture in time and understanding, the image of the shepherd seems the most fertile. The fisherman took from such a vast source that until recently we did not understand our connection to the lakes, rivers, and oceans. We are only now beginning to realize the depths of this intimate relationship: the whole is indeed part of us and us of it. Perhaps to begin an understanding of the person, we may return to the first image that presented itself to humankind as some significant frame of reference, one that spoke to the heart of the species: the shepherd, that responsible person who lived in some form of symbiosis with the whole.

The shepherd had a responsibility of the one to the many, of the many for the one. The flock needed tending and protection. The tribe needed the flock. The natural rhythms of seasons, of births and deaths – theirs and ours – bounded the reality of resource interface and gave a cadence to our presence. Now we cannot recapture those pastoral idyllic moments where grazing animals and playing children was all there was. It never was quite so simple. The wolf was always there, a hint of a connection to the process of being and our relationship to something beyond ourselves. It is indeed poetic that the wolf has become one of the icons for the current awareness of endangered species. Could this be a precursor to our own endangerment?

Questions have become imperatives that demand answers in our time. As we ponder extinctions and what we perceive as radical flora and fauna alterations, there seems to be a need for a balance, a rhythm of being that gives a holy time to each. We cannot create a static moment and protect others and ourselves from change, but we could allow ourselves the necessary time to grow and integrate both our individual and corporate presence into the current global moment. All of those inane questions: Do we need the Snail Darter, the Wolf, the Eagle, the Porpoise, and the Whale? These questions belie an understanding of us, much less anything else. We may recall Martin Heidegger's Being and Time and his mandate "to become shepherds of being."

Again, in that great bell curve of our present circumstance, the biodiversity is all here. Should we not be cognizant of this presence and attempt at least some sort of integration of being that gives to each their circumstance? Our hearts are touched (somewhat) by the starving children. Should our hearts also see the others in our time and should they not give us some pause? Perhaps this is that quantum leap of understanding that will bring the Truth of the Now into our focus. A pause that gives rise to … What is a person, an egg, a sperm, a zygote, a …? What is anything? Is everything not some measure of an eternal rhythm played by some infinite orchestra or are these just images of words that paint beyond our understanding? Maybe not, we may be thresholding here on a most profound truth.

Is there too little or too much? Are we too soon, too late, too … whatever? All are references to quantity and time. Change is time. Where does this leave us? All things change. We have no alternative but to accept change. So maybe we should own our participation in change. This would mandate an understanding of our relationship to time, to self and to the other. Where does this perspective on time leave us? Is it human time, geological time, universal time ...? This may seem too complex and yet, perhaps it is too simple for us to comprehend. What if all we need to do to understand our place in time is to slow down? What a simple statement and yet it is so pregnant with possibility.

Slow down! This could be a profound mandate. Is this all we need? Perhaps it is. If we were to eat more slowly, we would digest our food better, and eat less. Doing just this would make many people – the world – better off. I cannot think of anything that would not be better by slowing human activity down. We do not need to rush into or out of anything, except to respond to a fire or someone in danger. If we saw a natural catastrophe or an emergency, we would respond. There is no need to worry. We will not lessen our commitment to self and circumstance. If we would just slow down, we would be "at the ready" because we would have a clearer vision of an understanding of ourselves and our circumstance. If we did this we could listen to our children laugh and we could learn to laugh with them.

In order to do this, there is a need to start with a new kind of honesty. It cannot be a limiting kind of honesty. This would have to be a complete form of honesty that gives to each their due. Social science's descriptive efforts have, for the most part, failed. These descriptions have led us away from knowing ourselves as we relate to circumstance, painting society as some entity in and of itself. Society has become something to which blame can be attached. This new honesty needs to be an organic honesty that speaks to each individual's reality as it is integrated in time and space. We all need a place in the hierarchy of being and time where we own our current circumstance, while acquiring a rhythm that follows the seasons of life and of time. We need a gentle flow instead of a rush. We need to learn to stand still and be silent.

Concerned individuals who have been victimized through buying into the necessity of fast-paced economics, dual incomes, careers, and shooting stars as (successful?) models do not quite know what to let go of and what to hang on to. This slowing down to meet natural patterns would not lead to an economic collapse. Sunsets and moonrises do not take forever! If we all slowed down we would need less, use less, share more, and spend our time-being as a person in the process of growth and development by being who we really are as we move through the seasons of our lives. We would then be maturing with a natural flow of self towards the Truth and we would share our being and time with loved ones in the pursuit of real happiness, where fulfillment would be the definition of personhood. "How do we get out of the current being and time traps? Is it possible to get out of these traps?" Yes, it can be done.

Most of us just exist; we are working to stay even with our circumstance and we are not getting what we really need and want – to enjoy the seasons of life and of time. The enjoyment of self and circumstance provides real models where we can learn the full potential of what being a person is all about, by expanding an understanding of ourselves and our roles in the world, sharing feelings of joy and sadness, staying physically sound, and making a commitment to spiritual growth. This last ingredient is essential in providing values that ensure a maintained focus and an integration of the caring attributes of personhood that are displayed in every sharing human moment. Currently, the person's circumstance is a global commonality. We all share the same attribute of common desires – to share our being and time with our mates, our children, to be productive in some creative work, and to commune with friends.

To merely have the truth presented will not help some whose wounds have rendered them dysfunctional. They need another kind of help in healing and growth. A measure of this kind of help is actually essential in every person's life. We only maintain our classification as a member of the species by maintaining our social interface with each other. Sharing our being with other members of our kind is what makes us human. It also makes us honest.

Perhaps in our time we have to resort to a game in order to entertain ourselves, to discover ourselves and our relationship to others. If this is true, then it truly must be a game of Olympian proportions.

WARS OF THE MOMENT

For many in the U.S. population when the word *War* enters conversations – conversations for the most part not blessed with facts and reflective wisdom – there emerges a stance either for or against what is currently going on in Afghanistan and Iraq, as well as many other parts of the world. Many of the position-takings of the day are branded diatribes of left or right. So tell me, what color is close enough to mark our way towards an understanding of war?

The organic positioning on truths is the only one that matters for us. Truths that grow in depth and stature over time have no special color or flavor. Truth, as such, is a beacon allowing all who grow in wisdom to accept that which is part of a knowable now. The application of prudence to that acceptance is a given.

There are always befores and afters – antecedents – traces – winds of history – or caprice of the present. Yet, truth is not hidden in some dark cave. There are threads, webbing that pulls and holds ingredients in the boiling pot of time.

If we took time to understand, and if we looked at history, we could distill unjust wars' causes to four: *Fear, Anger, Guilt, and False Pride*. One could also mention the seven deadly sins, yet I think when sufficient reflection takes place, the four causes will do. The sins are subsumed therein. The upside to these four negative theaters of human involvement would be just wars driven by *Prudence, Survival, Appropriate Values, and Pride with Integrity.* For the most part, history's musty veil has obscured much of war's efforts. Or perhaps we have, in our hubris, ignored its teachings. To avoid the heaping of blame on others and on time, it may serve us well to focus on two of the wars currently underway.

We could for example start with 9/11; that act alone would be sufficient without all of the concomitant circumstances that harbored many hidden fires heating boiling pots of stew – racial, tribal, religious, economic, or some grand mixture of grudges and vendettas. All stews of history were banquets for beasts with victims: the former were those whose character was predisposed and war resulted, and the latter ranged, as always, from innocent to participant. Still, in the course of human events, notions of just and unjust wars were pinned to the sashes and lapels of warriors. From the menagerie of confrontations, seeds of hate and misunderstandings, along with a measure of wisdom, have been sown that were eventually distilled, addressed, and redressed, from whence emerged as formal components (condiments if you will) of war's meal: arbitrations, agreements, concords, treaties, just wars, surgical strikes, interventions, etc., all of which came to form the reasoned wills of most.

What tribe or people has not felt the sting of war? It seems endemic to the species, and yet the truth is that most of the human population has never participated directly in war. Life presents too many necessities and opportunities for commitments and creations to let destruction have its way. In time, laws and courts contribute to an acceptable venue, albeit incomplete, for the growth, the development, and the protection of humankind.

Questions of the present are these: Was Afghanistan a good place to start? And if so, is it a good place to finish? Was Iraq a good place to go? And if so, is it a good place to stay long enough to give the people of Iraq an opportunity to leap beyond their history of problematic tribal madness and enter a 21st-century world where opportunities abound for every person, be they man, woman, child, Kurd, Sunni, or Shia? The answer is a resounding yes! In addition, we must also remember the vast sea of Africans and Asians, so long forgotten.

Trouble follows trouble – warlords, drugs, the Taliban, criminals of every ilk – all need excising and the patients need healing. This is a healing from old wounds that have festered in environments that produced hatred and despair. To invite these people into the 21st-century family of nations – a family of nations that albeit has some individuals who do not exude a cosmopolitan attitude of global participation – will not be an easy thing to do. There will be conflict and the loss of life, and yet if we do not make a concerted effort to create opportunities for all nation states to gather sufficient expertise among their own to govern, protect, and grow, we are condemning them and us to the degradations, disruptions, and the deaths of war.

In the latter part of the 20th century, the United States has stood by long enough, and to its everlasting shame watched the deterioration of global circumstances. Was the moral outrage any different in Afghanistan and Iraq than in many other parts of the globe in the last half of the 20th century? No, it was not.

The omnipresent media, in its ever-growing fashion, has flourished sufficiently to provide an ongoing diet of information that has given the global family an opportunity to garner sufficient facts to make more mature and honest choices about the discrepancies that have become the catalysts for unrest and war. Now, with a critical mass of information and the ever-mounting troves of technology, we have finally come face to face with the lassitude and adolescent ignorance of the seeming sophisticates of the planet. The truth is now becoming such an integrated fact that it is impossible for any enlightened person to continue to stand by and watch the wanton suffering of so many members of the global family. That truth also contains sufficient information to give us the understanding that a zero sum game can be imagined only by the naïve. That sacrifices will be made of life and limb is a fact (see note, next page). Also, the fact that all of the people of the planet must share this loss has finally made itself manifest. We can no longer presume some sense of superiority and watch the death and suffering of the poor and subjugated by saying, "It's theirs, not ours!"

Sons and daughters – and *all* of us are sons and daughters – will continue to perish in the human drama. Our challenge is to make sure that each one is accounted for in some humane fashion, ensuring that their passing and their presence made a difference. This and this alone will justify our efforts. For all to have enough time and resources to make their mark in this grand play, on this grand stage, is the mandate of our time. We now know enough to take action, whether this action is the intervention in the affairs of a mad state, or of a mad mind, *the truth stays the same*: Own it now! Or bear the consequences. All things move, malevolent or otherwise, and we must commit to what we now know. Resting, or hiding, when we should be active and committed, does not get the job done. I might add that the verbal pontifications by those too timid to commit will not stop the tide of deaths that swell the shores of humankind.

The rash and less-than-civil discussions of the day should pale in the face of the truth of the now. We know enough to begin.

We know enough to commit. Now we must learn enough to honor those who have given their last measure in this great human epic. To belittle their sacrifices by turning our backs to the winds of change and opportunity is to spit in their faces and turn ourselves into non-caring consumers of capricious fancy and foible. Life matters and our appreciation of its heroics can only be measured by responsible commitments to us all.

The journey has already begun, the game is underway, and the choice is ours. This young maturing republic has a wealth of energy and creativity; what we now need is sufficient leadership to direct us towards a new and grand purpose, the purpose of the giving of our very best to others so that they too may enjoy the élan of life and its overflowing opportunities to create and to love.

NOTE: Any reasonable assessment of the military efforts in theater during conflict in Afghanistan and Iraq would have to conclude that there have been relatively small numbers of casualties for the Coalition forces. The numbers of wounded, as always, have been significant. However, the operational procedures to care for them, in both theater and elsewhere, have proven to be miraculous. We are creating a new history in these wars and it must be noted that our effort to care for our warriors reflects a deep level of conscious effort and commitment in deployments as well as in aftercare. Finally, we are arriving at a level of understanding that bespeaks an awareness of the value for all human life.

You may also wish to see "Strike Force" as well as a few others, like "Kosovo Manifesto," "On Gazing at a Maple Tree in Spring," and "The Battle," along with other poems of war, conflict, and the value of human life, all life, in *Always Extolling*.

WHAT IS RIGHT?

What is right? What are we talking about? Where is it? When is it important? These are all questions that have entered upon a new age, an age of oxymoronic speech, where if we were to say "It all depends" – "It's all relative, isn't it?" – most would feel quite politically correct. Yet we know that some things can't be just brushed away. We also must know when we answer questions with more questions that there is the possibility that we have started to reflect. However, when they become rhetorical questions, because we choose not to care, or even to not want to know, we are in trouble.

We all know there are some truths that are really important, some truths that cannot be taken for granted. Yet, we all do. Life is a process with precursors, concomitant circumstances, and necessary conditions. There is always a before and an after. We ignore these surrounding circumstances at our peril. Health care awareness has currently reached an apogee never before available to humankind. Ortega y Gassett's profound declaration – "*Yo soy yo y mi circunstancia, y si no la salvo a ella no me salvo yo*" (I am myself and my circumstance and if I do not save it [my circumstance] I do not save myself) – is now almost a century old. This dawning of awareness is now becoming an essential point of departure in our consideration of everything. Our current level of comprehension and integration is evolution's most valuable gift.

We do, however, remain anthropocentric, myopically so, and we still are very naïve about the interconnectedness of everything. We maintain this ignorance at our own risk and the risking of all life. To be responsible for what we know is always our most fundamental choice.

Currently, lives are being lived in which we say we are paying attention. A brief reflection says, "No traffic accidents – some close calls though," and we move on to something else. Too often we do not get deep enough to garner really meaningful data. A song on the radio, some talk show host or their interviewee, grabs our attention, or we allow ourselves to be assaulted by a never-ending series of explosive montages of sight and sound, and we float from one thing to another without mining the depths of many given subjects for their consistency of logic, or for any personally meaningful connection.

I used to ask my students, "Who is the most important person in the world for you?" Few would say, "I am!" Yet when it was pointed out to them that it had to be the self (even if we were in the act of self-sacrifice for the benefit of another, or others), they still had difficulty focusing on this truth. Seldom do we confuse ourselves with another. There are those, however, who spend inordinate amounts of time trying to be someone else, or in the acceptably shallow language of the day, "act like someone."

Ortega actually warned against this too as an error of perspective. There is only one of each of us. Most individuals, and I would hazard that this is now a very large number, have moved in their perception of their interface with existence from an "in here" to an "out there." While this is indispensable to our binary point of departure, there must be a reasoned balance. More now than ever, we are engaged in an interface that is not an efficacious blend of a "here now" mixed with a healthy "if then." Many now spend much of their time "ahead" of themselves. This orientation, for the most part, is a "disconnected with the future," a "not there yet" point of view. If we at least knew something about where we have been and where we were going, it would be helpful. Our ability to have practical, doable dreams also seems to be waning.

Too many younger and older individuals want a lifestyle that requires a substantial focus-over-time in order to achieve, much less maintain, what they think they want. It is well known that if we live "out there" too long we lose contact with the richness of the present. We all need a now filled with capricious displays of thunder, downpours, storms of all kinds, and hazy days with gentle winds that fill our memory banks and feed our souls. This is indispensable to balancing human life. Too many of us are losing opportunities to enjoy the screen of the present while anxiously anticipating coming attractions.

There is some poetry in all of this. The technology of the age (TVs and cell phones) gives us an omnipresent that allows us to not be present. Many have become just observers and listeners. Many have given away their sacred right to create, to participate in an interface that feeds the satisfactions of mind, body, emotions, and soul. We rob ourselves of an "in here" orientation that if owned gives us access to not only a reflecting repose that distills in its fathoming wheat from chaff, but also opens vistas to the depths of our talents and pulls out of us what is eternally already there. It is in the process of self-discovery, self-ownership, and the sharing of that discovery that we find our truly human selves.

As we "reason" our way to rationalizations of our current circumstance, do we snag ourselves on perches that proclaim there are no "relative truths" or "universal truths" that can be used as a template for an operation through which we could base our perceptions of truth? In this postmodern world, I am of the opinion that we can come close enough to the truth, in most cases, to be able to determine what is right. The exceptions would be few and even then somewhat understandable. In those cases where we really don't know what to do we can take time to reflect, or to study our way to an acceptable solution. We all know there are emergencies that demand an immediate response, and yet even when they occur we respond better when prepared and with some measure of reflection.

We need to be honest enough to own the best of our humanity as it has made itself manifest to us over time. We cannot coast and spend most of our time as observers and listeners. Life demands an active participation based upon an understanding of all available knowledge. The problem of human existence has always been a tug of war between avarice and wisdom. Too much of anything, especially if it is not ours, or needed, inhibits the enjoyment of ourselves and of all other things. Gaining wisdom must be an ever-present commitment to integrity. If something presents itself as true, our responsibility must be to incorporate that truth in our personal and worldview as we continue to move towards some ever more comprehensible present.

We also must know it is not enough to "know." We have to practice what we know. The most dangerous state of affairs is to "*think we know*" and do nothing. Current "lifestyles" are saturated with behaviors that belie our supposed sophistication. We can only own what we know by exercising what we know. To be truly human we must do our truths. How many smokers, when asked if they know it is not in their best interests to smoke, say, "I know." What do they know? Not enough to incorporate what they think they know into a life-saving decision, a decision that is made not only for themselves, but also for their children as well as all others.

Postmodern lifestyles are replete with examples of this kind. When the obvious is apparent, some still choose not to own it. This is not a smart thing, a cool thing, or a hot thing. It is a stupid thing. Too many individuals wear their ignorance as if it were a badge of courage. To be fully human we must want the truth, and in having the truth, truly possessing it, we become who we already are. That is close enough to really Holy Stuff.

You may also like to see *The Concept of Personhood in the Evolutionary Process of Being.*

AN AGENDA FOR US ALL

Is a part of our purpose to acknowledge our presence in ways that complement the whole? Are we here to make some sharing commitment to those with whom we make life's journey? Answers to these fundamental questions are what we should be about, not only for ourselves, but also for the most precious of all—our children. What obligations do we have to them, and to others? At the very least, we must be obligated to a "Touching" that says, "Yes to self, and yes to life."

As we raise our babes to toddlers and then to preschoolers and finally to scholars, what purpose do we see being fulfilled as they trek from home to school and thereabouts for some 16 years? Are we confident that the schools and our home environs have provided the essentials for making the significant life choices that we all must make? Did it provide us with all we needed to know to subdue the formidable passions and challenges of our times? The qualified answer to this is yes, because if for no other reason we are here now. However, this hardly answers the question. What are we doing to curb drug trafficking, slavery, abuse of all kinds? What have we done to quash malignant despots and dictators? How often have we stepped in to stop the genocides on the planet?

We fully comprehend that there have been surprises along the way as well as inherent blind spots. This does not mean that we can exonerate ourselves. Serious pitfalls and obstacles have left scars upon the souls of humanity, scars that must now be dealt with by this current generation for our sake and for the sake of our children. Will their life experiences and the informal as well as the formal education we gave them provide the necessary tools to make those new and difficult choices for themselves and for all the rest of us?

This will be most difficult unless we give them concrete working examples of involvement. Perennial questions always shadow every society and the educational infrastructure of any society. No group of people is sacrosanct. Nothing is perfect. Yet History, being the great teacher that she is, has continued to provide us with reflective pieces of time's mosaic. In some cases, we have paid too little attention to the patterns of our footsteps.

Having taught and counseled for some 40 years, I have often wondered as each new group of students passed before me either in the classrooms, or on the schoolyards, in the halls, on the campuses, or wherever ... Are we doing all that we should be doing? Are they ready for this semester? How well has someone else done his or her job in order for me to do mine? Are we getting better at recognizing the precursors of catastrophes? The record here too is slipshod: Yes, we have improved in some areas, but ignored others, botched opportunities to nip malignancies in the bud, and praised too little as well as too much.

With each passing year, I have felt there could be a more inclusive and comprehensive way to teach reading, to teach logic, to teach ethics, and the other essentials of a broad and significant curriculum. I even wondered if the curriculum was too broad. Do we have to know something about everything, or, as they say, "Is learning how to learn the real key?" Is education just a patchwork quilt of some of this and some of that? In addition, just how eclectic can we be and still have sufficient understanding to fathom our presence in a 21st-century global whole? "Just teach them to use a computer!" some say. The mechanics are at times daunting and the content can be challenging. Some of the fare is incredibly boring and some even noxious. So, is that what education is currently about? Steve Jobs (founder of Apple) has finally said he was not sure a computer for each child was going to get the job done. I emphatically agree.

To what purpose should we put our efforts towards our most precious treasures – our children? How could we give them an opportunity to better participate in life's great undertakings while helping them to prepare to reap the benefits of life's offerings? Each new day is full of purpose, a purpose that allows for a giving of one's self to one's self so creative juices can flow and they can share their presences with others. How can we help them to prepare themselves for these gifts of life – a life that will present them with opportunities to laugh, to cry, to wonder, and to create?

That education can be a blessing or a curse can be hotly debated. The scholarly effort on both sides has beaten the educational horse in both an attempt to kill it and an attempt to drive it forward. All movements have precursors, of deaths, of births, and of transformations. I stand on the side of nurturing an education, *educere*, a leading out of one so that that one can be shared with the many, so that all may participate in the gifts of creation. I firmly believe it is a great challenge and a marvelous opportunity to participate in the growth of our understanding and the application of that understanding to our current moment.

So what are some of those profoundly simple things that would provide our children with a more comprehensive educational experience, including better reading and comprehension? Who has any doubts? Is some fundamental understanding of mathematics important? This is beyond any doubt. An appreciation of logic, ethics, aesthetics, and history is crucial. The sadness of the day is, who could even tell you what they are? The Trivium and Quadrivium have given way to an accumulation of petty nuances that flavor socially scorched or overly sweetened sentiments.

The manner in which one gets one's education and the application of that education is always of paramount importance. Are we really the rational social animal, a homofaber, a destroyer, a creator of symbols, a freedom lover, and a soul-seeking, sentient being? Is there a benefit to having some universal point of departure that while keeping us focused also points the way with sufficient reflective repose to new and better things? I firmly believe there is.

Let us look at the old 80/20 rule: That is, 80 percent of things are doing just fine the way they are, and 20 percent need some gentle, or forceful, tweaking. We need to follow Nature's path, a gentle touch here, a smack there. We must never forget the presence of the Eternal Hand.[*]

The history of our presence can only be understood and revered when we accept the incredible benevolence of the process of growth. If we reflect on history, we will see that all changes stood on the shoulders of some current infrastructure. Wisdom also tells us that one degree of change over time will place us in a very different space. With this in mind, we should all labor faithfully with the utmost integrity and live lovingly for the greater good of us all.

---

[*] See also "Communication," "The Hand Upon My Shoulder," "Messages," and "Just a Touch" in *Through the Swamps of Time*.

THE UNITED NATIONS

A Brief Critique and Some Observations

One Side of the Coin

The United Nations (UN) was born amidst the rubble and ashes of war. A panting world saw a new need and set sail upon a sea of intended understanding and sharing. How well are we doing sixty-plus years into the undertaking? No pun intended. What has this organization, wrought with such intent and hope, accomplished? Many nations have joined that first cadre of naïve and hopeful statesmen and bureaucrats, representatives for the most part of fledgling nations wanting so much to have a say in taking, giving, and sharing. There is always the "other side" of every effort, and with the UN there are no exceptions. Greed and corruption are that other side of every human interchange.

The intervening years have taken the luster off the shine of hope. Struggles were attempted and forgotten. Learning curves were steep and many of the unwilling were sucked into that old bow of corruption. "If you wash my feet, I will wash your hands" became the mantra of avarice, of ignorance, of convenience. Aspects of the UN that were hoped to be the pinnacle of human progress rapidly degenerated into a cauldron of the worst of bureaucratic finagling. Power-hungry and greedy secretaries and ambassadors preyed upon the less able, others begged from the more affluent, and many stood by as spectators.

A limiting Security Council's perspective that limps along with just a one-vote veto barring action has not met the needs of an imploding world. Where and when military expertise and might were needed, they were not employed. In a universal act of cowardice, the members deferred to an organization that was neither ready nor able to act, and in their deferring, adopted sanctimonious airs of cooperation. A simplistic "theirs, not mine" attitude became the common call blanketed by the amorphous and nebulous phrases of "internal affairs," "meddling," and "sanctions." Then, in the midst of this membership of mutual and cooperative responsibility, the members turned their backs on each other.

A universal declaration of human rights was written and then was shelved in place of the nefarious policy of the sanctimony of a nation's internal affairs. "Slaughter, rape, maim, and wreak mayhem if you must, just don't do it by crossing borders," was the understood *modus operandi*. Such lack of courage was and is a paltry commitment to the obvious truths of the current age. These actions are more than shameful. They are cruel, despicable, and unforgivable. Words devoid of action become whispers lost in tinkling glasses of diplomatic socials. Raging cries and screams were seen as repeatedly crying wolf. Too few chose to listen to the victims of starvation, genocide, massacres, rapes, and terror.

Wars have come and gone while the seemingly eternal institutionalized conflicts of righteousness confronted bigotry and ignorance. The invisible "theys" of the hinterlands and urban centers were marginalized or co-opted in forgotten or brutalized fashion by the many. Economics birthed plenty for some, and subjugated and stunted innate freedoms in others.

To have shouldered the communal responsibility of educating to ameliorate the insidious racialists, extremisms, dogmatisms, and hypocrisies would have been helpful. To have fostered and abetted the corruption of a base sense of power grabbing and a despicable lack of caring for the benefit of others is unpardonable.

Diplomacy degenerated into that worst kind of stasis while becoming the "Great Game" of the day. "Sanctions," never quite enforceable, became the pastime of wranglers, liars, cheats, and cowards. Secretaries assumed positions that were never fashioned for such assumption of management, or mismanagement. That there has not been in recent years the needed leadership and honest growth and development of a multicultural, transnational body is a sad commentary on the lack of sustained commitment to the betterment of humankind. This failure of maturity and general lack of a sense of purpose must be duly acknowledged.

The Other Side of the Coin

It must be said that there always have been, among the maddening herds, statesmen and honest men of conscience and social purpose. Truths of human needs and common denominators have been set in oral and written traditions from the advent of "more than one." Agreements, accords and concords, treaties, edicts, documents of every ilk have been available to those who cared enough to search, to study, and to share in open dialogue that honest interchange of ideas and beliefs – those secular and saintly standpoints that have become the great pedestals of human achievement and advancement. All this was shared in special enclaves in fits and starts as growth and understanding, so essential to the well-being of the species, progressed over time.

Meanwhile, in shadowed doorways and narrow passageways, from tall buildings, plains, and urban jungles, from every corner of the globe, smiles graced faces and gentle gestures acknowledged brothers and sisters. Media elevated, assuaged, and assaulted the dignity of the species. Yet a communion of mutual understanding and compassion has maintained its committed and gentle presence, shedding grace upon the human family.

The recent plethora of multinationals has served to enhance as well as subjugate the spirit of humankind. Every one of them must revisit their innate corporate and communal responsibility: if to one, then to all. Yet in the wake of the species' movement, we still see awash the fragile, the harmed, the destitute, and the enslaved.

Yes, there have been those stellar moments when refugees were protected and fed. Yes, there have been those medical miracles of disease suppression. Yes, there has been assistance given after disasters. In addition, yes, we have had a modicum of success in spreading common values. Still, in all of this, we have not done enough to understand, to care for, to be responsible for, and to respect the righteousness of human values in every corner, at every task. We must raise our voices in joyous hope and bend our shoulders to every opportunity to recognize universal truths. In the owning of these universal truths, we all must be proactive in our commitment to protect anyone and everyone in that complementing embrace of humanity, regardless of national boundaries that give rise to subjugation, or legalistic nonsense that does almost nothing to protect human rights. It has always been the spirit inherent in natural law that has preceded the letter of any law. It is to the former that we owe our eternal and everlasting commitment.

Our most important responsibility is to shape the human interface and give direction to the movement of humankind. This falls to each and every one of us, and certainly not just in our personal lives, but also in our familial, communal, national, and global lives. As an age of interdependence has swept the globe, a lack of individual and communal trust has also permeated our understanding, or lack thereof. We have entered an age in which an isolationism of fear separates not only countries from each other, but members of families from each other and individuals from one another, as well as individuals from themselves.

Courage must mount the steed and with a caring heart, we must apply ourselves by joining in a commitment to an integration of available resources and organizational wherewithal to achieve the essential needs of the global community. In committing to do this we must seek sweeping reorganization of the UN by having an international committee, a group of the highest integrity, undertake the identification of any and all opportunists and the prosecution in the International Court of Criminal Justice of every single criminal activity connected with the UN, or any participating government. This would send a precedent-setting message that no one is above the law and enforcement of the rule of law. Reinforcing the fact that the exercising of the rule of law is one of the primary prerequisites for order and planned development, achievable over time, is of paramount importance.

Our efforts must be to always present a moving protective responsibility, one that targets the endemic corruptness of all global entities, whether these are multinational corporations, governments, or organizations. How can one expect to exert influence when the body politic of the ever more international organizations is colored with base, degrading behavior that brings out the very worst of humankind?

The time has come for a fundamental form of integrity that embodies action, an action born by an awareness of an understanding that inserts itself in every human interchange, a legitimacy of purpose that complements the events of evolution and gives a sense of belonging, one to the other, to each and every person as a natural right of being. We cannot continue on our merry ways by ignoring neighbors who live in squalor, deprivation, and suffering when we know that these conditions become the enclaves of depression and explosion. We must be aware, as a whole, of inherent potential rights in every human being: the right to life, liberty, work, and the pursuit of happiness.

Postscript: A Suggestion

There has been an incredible lack of understanding of the human necessity in the use of strength to implement goals and development by dealing swiftly with obstructionists. Along with murderers, rapists, and pillagers, this has been the hallmark of a lack of sufficient focus on human potential; we must now continue to deal with the problem of the use of force in solving human problems. While many shirked their responsibilities to their fellows, they met in congenial discussion going almost nowhere and accomplishing far too little. A suggestion is made here to work towards a merging of NATO, CSTO, SEATO, and any other willing coalition of forces. This would be the beginning of a global enforcement potential, eventually encompassing every nation, once they have the economic wherewithal to assume such an obligation. The objective would be a global organization charged with the responsibility to intervene in any armed conflict with a policing authority charged with the responsibility to establish a social environment that once established would assume, if it can, its own policing activity. The expressed purpose would be to stop the slaughter of innocents and to achieve a stability that benefits the general populace and any nation's ability to maintain its productive involvement in the international community. A governing board of the participating nations would be charged with the responsibility to act with a majority of 80 percent. If any nation refuses in any consecutive two mobilizations, their participation in offensive and defensive involvement would be seen as a humiliation of that nation, and every other nation would enforce an economic sanction commensurate with that nation's participating responsibility.

There is some number of nations that cannot participate, either in personnel or in economic aid, in such an effort. In those cases, the goal would be for the participating nations to create an individual and social environment within that nation, along with the economic infrastructure to support the nation, so that a sense of stability could provide for a productive window of opportunity for that nation. Starting now, and for the foreseeable future, no nation can choose to absent itself from the internal and international responsibility of cooperation in the global well-being of all of the world's people. Revolution and disruptions, as well as madness of the masses, can occur at any time and in any place. The family of humankind must stand ready to ameliorate the efforts of corruption and destruction wherever they occur.

A group of like-minded nations must be charged with the responsibility to stop any and all assaults on humanity's rights and the limiting of its potential. This must be accomplished without having to wait upon the procrastination of a muddling group of bureaucrats who know next to nothing of leadership in conflict, or the need to act with some dispatch when life is at risk. Let it be resolved that the global community will not sit idly by, as they have in the last half of the 20th century, while people are sacrificed on an altar of ignorance and procrastination.

You may be interested in the poems in *Always Extolling*. Some twenty of the selected poems deal with human understanding and the need to honestly own our humanity.

www.ingramcontent.com/pod-product-compliance
Lightning Source LLC
Chambersburg PA
CBHW051812040426
42446CB00007B/637